T0360642

Intuitive Expertise and Financial Decision-Making

This book provides insights into the hidden role of intuitive expertise in financial decision-making. The authors show and discuss how expertise combined with intuitive judgments positively affect decision-making outcomes.

The book builds on the latest academic studies in this emergent field. In combination with the academic perspective, the authors provide a field study that they conducted in the context of mergers and acquisitions (M&As), a common and critical strategic investment for companies. The interviews were carried out with experts and decision-makers in large and successful international companies (i.e., M&A experts, CEOs, CFOs, and board members). The book provides a solid theoretical and empirically based grounding of the topic. In addition, it offers suggestions to practitioners on how they can develop and nurture intuitive expertise in strategic investment decision-making. The report of the field study provides examples and quotes from interviews to visualize findings, thus helping practitioners gain understanding and insights from the text. The authors also discuss the downsides of intuitive expertise, such as biases and flawed decision-making.

For scholars, students, and professionals, the book offers a concise and up-to-date summary of an emergent stream of research, exploring how cognition and judgment affect financial decision-making.

Michael Grant earned his PhD at Uppsala University and the Department of Business Studies, where he holds the position as Senior Lecturer. In his research, he focuses on expertise and experts' use of intuition in complex tasks, such as strategic decision-making. Furthermore, he has a broad research interest in M&As. In addition, he has more than 20 years of extensive experience working internationally with M&As. Michael has published his research in book chapters (Routledge, Edward Elgar) and the *British Accounting Review*. He is an executive board member of the Swedish Academy of Auditing.

Fredrik Nilsson has been Professor of Business Studies, specializing in Accounting at Uppsala University since 2010. Previously, he was Professor of Economic Information Systems at Linköping University. In his research, he focuses on how different information systems (e.g., related to financial accounting, management control, and risk management) are designed and used in formulating and implementing strategies. Fredrik has published his research in books (e.g., Routledge and Springer) and in scientific journals (e.g., *Accounting & Finance*, the *British Accounting Review, British Journal of Management, European Management Journal, Management Accounting Research*, and *Scandinavian Journal of Management*). He is Chairman of the Swedish Academy of Auditing and Chairman of the Swedish Research School of Management and Information Technology.

Routledge Focus on Accounting and Auditing

Advances in the fields of accounting and auditing as areas of research and education, alongside shifts in the global economy present a constantly shifting environment. This presents challenges for scholars and practitioners trying to keep up with the latest important insights in both theory and professional practice. Routledge Focus on Accounting and Auditing presents concise texts on key topics in the world of accounting research.

Individually, each title in the series provides coverage of a key topic in accounting and auditing, whilst collectively, the series forms a comprehensive collection across the discipline of accounting.

Deleuze and Guattarí Perspectives
Niels Joseph Lennon

Public Sector Audit
David C. Hay and Carolyn J. Cordery

Corporate Governance and Integrated Reporting
Boards, Long-Term Value Creation, and the New Accountability
Laura Girella

Budgeting and Performance Management in the Public Sector
Sara Giovanna Mauro

Intuitive Expertise and Financial Decision-Making
Michael Grant and Fredrik Nilsson

For more information about this series, please visit: www.routledge.com/Routledge-Focus-on-Accounting-and-Auditing/book-series/RFAA

Intuitive Expertise and Financial Decision-Making

Michael Grant
Fredrik Nilsson

Routledge
Taylor & Francis Group

LONDON AND NEW YORK

First published 2023
by Routledge
4 Park Square, Milton Park, Abingdon, Oxon OX14 4RN

and by Routledge
605 Third Avenue, New York, NY 10158

Routledge is an imprint of the Taylor & Francis Group, an informa business

British Library Cataloguing-in-Publication Data
A catalogue record for this book is available from the British Library

ISBN: 978-0-367-47662-5 (hbk)
ISBN: 978-1-032-36175-8 (pbk)
ISBN: 978-1-003-03572-5 (ebk)

DOI: 10.4324/9781003035725

Typeset in Times New Roman
by codeMantra

Contents

Preface

Financial decisions have a significant impact on companies' ability to successfully implement corporate and business strategies. These types of decisions are often related to risky and long-term investments. Examples of these are investments in research and development programs, new technologies, or mergers and acquisitions (M&As). In this book, the focus is on M&As.

A decision to make a strategic investment is almost always complex, and there is seldom only one way to judge it, besides the fact that the investment will affect the company for a long time and that it concerns an uncertain future. In order to handle uncertainty, models and tools are used, for example, discounted cash flow or SWOT analysis. However, we believe that the importance of these is exaggerated and can be misleading. In the end, financial decision-making is about judgments and decisions by people.

This book focuses on senior executives and their use of intuitive expertise in financial judgments and decisions. We are fascinated by how intuitive expertise is used in business and especially in financial decision-making. It started with one of us writing a PhD dissertation on making acquisitions (Grant, 2018). One of the essays was further developed and eventually published in the *British Accounting Review* (Grant & Nilsson, 2020). This paper was followed by a book chapter in an edited volume on intuition research (Grant et al., 2020).

We started working on the present book in 2021. It builds on, and extends, our earlier work. For us it represents a significant step forward since it consolidates research from three fields of research: accounting, management, and psychology. We have also conducted interviews with senior executives. This rich theoretical and empirical material relates to financial decision-making and especially M&As. Our ambition is to provide the reader with a concise overview of the research frontier and provide new empirical insights.

We thank Professor Nils Brunsson and Associate Professor Jan Lindvall at the Department of Business Studies at Uppsala University for their valuable comments on the manuscript. Furthermore, we are grateful for comments on Chapter 2, provided by participants at the internal research conference at the Department of Business Studies at Uppsala University. We also thank Associate Professor Anna-Carin Nordvall at Uppsala University for support in conducting some of the interviews for the empirical study.

References

Grant, M. (2018). *Making acquisitions.* Ph.D. Dissertation. Department of Business Studies, Uppsala University.

Grant, M., & Nilsson, F. (2020). The production of strategic and financial rationales in capital investments: Judgments based on intuitive expertise. *British Accounting Review*, *52*(3), 100861.

Grant, M., Nilsson, F., & Nordvall, A. C. (2020). The use of intuitive expertise in acquisition-making: An explorative study. In Sinclair, M. (Ed.). *Handbook of Intuition Research as Practice* (pp. 39–55). Cheltenham: Edward Elgar Publishing.

1 Introduction

This book is about the concept of intuitive expertise—what it is, how it works, and how it is used in financial judgments and decisions. When discussing financial decision-making there is a tendency, among both scholars and practitioners, to focus on structures and processes such as models and tools. Less interest is directed toward the managers who judge and decide. Even when the focus is on how managers make financial decisions, it is described as a slow and rational process and more seldom as a process that is unconscious and intuitive (see Kahneman & Klein, 2009). Not surprisingly, a lot of interest and effort is put into refining the design and use of models for evaluating investments such as discounted cash-flow analysis and schemes for evaluating strategic fit. Many scholars and practitioners even believe that new and advanced information technology solutions, such as artificial intelligence (AI), can be a possible replacement for expert decision-makers in fields such as finance, accounting, and auditing.

This book presents a different perspective. Our focus is on the intuition and expertise that senior executives use when making financial decisions. Hence, the organizational and social context is not our main interest. More specifically, we provide a framework for intuitive expertise by examining the individual concepts intuition and expertise first separately and then jointly as intuitive expertise. This framework is related to decision-making by high-performing senior executives in large and successful companies. It builds on research from the fields of accounting, management, and psychology and we argue that these senior executives possess a type of unique knowledge that has been developed over a long period of time (Akinci & Sadler-Smith, 2012; Ericsson et al., 2006; Grant & Nilsson, 2020; Grant et al., 2020). This knowledge is defined as expertise and is often used in an unconscious manner, that is, even the expert can be unaware of its existence. Thus, it is intuitive and sometimes hidden. However, an expert's performance is highly visible.

DOI: 10.4324/9781003035725-1

A salient task of senior executives—perhaps the most important—is financial decision-making. In this book, we predominantly discuss the type of financial decisions that have a large and long-term impact on a company. These decisions also have a significant impact on the possibility of attaining the overall and most important objectives of the company. Hence, the decisions can be characterized as strategic. Examples of strategic decisions are investments in R&D, new plants, divestments, and acquisitions. In many companies, acquisitions constitute their largest investment, in fact, larger than both investments in R&D and capital expenditure (Mauboussin et al., 2016). Thus, for the senior executive, it is often the most important financial decision. The reasons are many. For example, acquisitions can be used to expand product and service portfolios and geographic reach. They can also provide swift access to technologies that are important in R&D activities. In this book, we focus on acquisitions since they play such an important role in financial decision-making and because they rely heavily on expertise. In addition, we will also discuss some other types of strategic decisions such as credit assessment and evaluation of start-ups. What all of these decisions have in common is that they are very complex. Because of this complexity, there are many different ways to judge them and to make decisions. There is simply no optimal solution.

This book provides the reader with an overview of the latest research in the fields of expertise and intuition. We do not claim that this overview is exhaustive, but it will give the reader insights from management, organization, and psychology studies. In addition, the overview covers relevant studies of financial decision-making in acquisitions. We have also conducted an empirical study of 12 senior executives and their use of intuitive expertise in financial decision-making.[1] The empirical study uses the literature review as its theoretical starting point, complementing and extending earlier research in the area. This interview-based study gives insights into characteristics, development and use of intuitive expertise, areas of expertise, and the articulation of intuition.

1.1 Intuitive expertise

Decision-making is often characterized as a process that requires rational analysis. A decision is made only after considering (all) possible alternatives and likely outcomes. Playing chess could seem to be an excellent example of this. However, the current chess world champion, Magnus Carlsen (2020), would probably not agree, as illustrated by the following quote:

As a rule, when I get to a position on the board, I have an idea of what I want to do and it usually comes quickly . . . it feels better, more harmonious, more in my style . . . it is subjective, with a lot of intuition.

Carlsen explains how he determines his next move. The idea comes up quickly, is not produced by conscious reasoning, and involves emotions. This clearly illustrates the use of intuitive expertise and offers insights into how it can be characterized. However, the lack of conscious analytical thinking in this quote is probably a surprise to many who are not expert chess players. Nevertheless, the thinking of professional chess players formed the starting point for studies of intuitive expertise[2] (Chase & Simon, 1973; De Groot, 1946/1978). Based on these studies, the management scholar and Nobel laureate, Herbert Simon (1992, p. 155) portrayed intuitive expertise as recognition:

The situation has provided a cue; this cue has given the expert access to information stored in memory, and the information provides the answer. Intuition is nothing more and nothing less than recognition.

Even though there were a few and important studies, researchers' interest in the area of intuitive expertise was limited until the early years of the new millennium. At that point in time, the concept was acknowledged in the fields of both psychology and management (Akinci & Sadler-Smith, 2012; Hodgkinson et al., 2008).

Today, intuition (Dane & Pratt, 2007; Sinclair, 2011) and expertise (Ericsson et al., 2006; Ward et al., 2020) have developed as two relatively separate research streams. However, the field of intuition also integrates findings from research on expertise (e.g., Dane & Pratt, 2007). The figure below illustrates research in the areas of intuition and expertise, with the intersection showing intuitive expertise. In the following three chapters, the terms in Figure 1.1. are defined and discussed: "expertise" in Chapter 2, "intuition" in Chapter 3, and "intuitive expertise" in Chapter 4.

1.2 Financial decision-making

Following Mintzberg et al., we use a classical definition of decision-making as the activities and events leading up to the commitment of action (Mintzberg et al., 1976). To be more specific and relating decision-making to the financial aspects of an acquisition, our interest is directed toward the activities and events leading up to the closing, or legal completion of an acquisition (Grant, 2018). Such a decision is typically materialized in a formal board decision and the signing

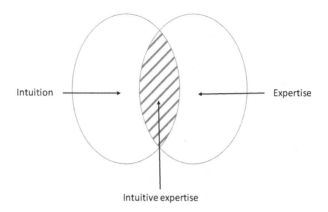

Figure 1.1 Intuitive expertise (adapted from Salas et al., 2010, p. 945).

of a sale purchase agreement followed by the fulfillment of closing conditions and transfer of the business to the acquirer. Consequently, we view financial decision-making not as the formal board decision, but as a process taking place over a longer period, typically several months or years, encompassing a myriad of judgments and decisions.

Throughout the book, we separate the terms "judgment" and "decision" for analytical and pedagogical reasons. Judgment is about making an evaluation, whereas a decision is defined as a choice between two or more alternatives (APA). However, this separation can be difficult to make in practice since a decision is preceded by a judgment, that is, an evaluation, of one or several alternatives. We call the person who makes the judgment, and eventually the decision, a decision-maker. Furthermore, the focus is on successful decision-makers, that is, high-performing senior executives, since they can be expected to be experts in their field.

We are especially interested in how these decision-makers use intuitive expertise. The reason is that the expert's knowledge is often hidden, even for the expert. Polanyi (1966/2009, p. 4) describes it as how "we can know more than we can tell" and uses the term "tacit knowledge." Following Polanyi, Tsoukas (2003, p. 410) describes the nature of tacit knowledge as "[t]acit knowledge cannot be 'captured', 'translated', or 'converted' but only displayed and manifested, in what we do." In line with this, the use of intuitive expertise is, arguably, to display tacit knowledge. We also know that experts, to a great extent, use and rely on intuitive expertise, especially when solving complex problems with myriads of solutions, a typical characteristic of financial decisions.

In the normative literature, financial decisions are often portrayed as being highly rational, following a linear mode of analysis (see for example, Koller et al., 2015). A lot of emphasis is placed on data quality and the calculation model(s) used for analysis. The assumption is that a high-quality decision can be made if the models and tools for making a financial decision are well designed. This is especially true for financial decisions of a strategic nature, such as pursuing an acquisition or a merger. The critical literature takes the opposite stance and has long discussed the design and use of these forms of rational decision-making with great skepticism (Mintzberg, 2000). Both positions have support in the literature and have also led to fierce debates.

Interestingly, the rational paradigm of decision-making has a solid position in teaching and research as well as in practice. Hence, it is difficult to argue that models and tools are not used or lack usefulness. At the same time, many of their weaknesses are not denied even by those who defend them. To us, and many other researchers, this constitutes a puzzle that is difficult to resolve. Obviously, some significant aspects of financial decision-making are missing, and we argue that one vital aspect is the role of intuitive expertise. In this vibrant field of research, there is a shift from studying the models and tools in decision-making to studying how high-performing individuals make judgments and decisions. A recent case study by us is representative of this stream of research (Grant & Nilsson, 2020). The quote below gives an insight into our main findings, for example, that the capital investment processes consisted of two parts with quite different characteristics (ibid., p. 2):

> *The case study shows that capital investment processes consist of two parts. The first part is the production of strategic and financial rationales. It is based on judgments of a myriad of factors and data concretized into rough estimates of how the acquisition is expected to affect value creation. Surprisingly, the process is without any visible analytical reasoning. Concepts and tools for strategic and financial analysis do not seem to be very important. Instead, judgments affecting the production of strategic and financial rationales largely follow an intuitive process based on expertise (see Kahneman & Klein, 2009). The second part consists of the presentation of strategic and financial rationales in approval documents. These rationales are logical and can be explained by analytical reasoning.*

One of the conclusions from our case study was that models and tools are not as important as might be expected. Much more significance was given to how the experts judge the myriad of factors that can affect the outcome of the acquisition. The experts judge what to include in the strategic and financial analysis, forming the rationales for making the acquisition. When presenting these rationales, concepts and tools are used. The documents and presentations provided to decision-makers are logical and analytically coherent with detailed calculations of future financial impacts and values. However, beneath the surface of the presentations, there can be a myriad of problems. Hence, the business case for an acquisition, or any strategic investment decision, can be framed and presented in different analytical ways depending on what those producing and presenting the business case want to achieve.

Even though it is interesting to discuss the relationship between the use of models and tools on the one hand and intuitive expertise on the other hand, this book focuses on the individual expert and how intuitive expertise is used in financial decision-making. We believe that such a focus adds more to our understanding of how judgments and decisions are made than further scrutinizing the role of models and tools. For this reason, though firmly rooted in the field of management, accounting, and finance, a large part of the content is dedicated to fundamental studies in the areas of expertise, intuition, and intuitive expertise.

1.3 A guide to the reader

This book provides insights into the hidden role of intuitive expertise in financial decision-making. In short, the book contributes to this emergent stream of research in two ways. First, we define and develop the concept of intuitive expertise by drawing on and consolidating some of the most important research in the area. Second, we investigate the role of intuitive expertise in financial decision-making by analyzing earlier field studies as well as conducting a field study that builds and adds to these insights. This new field study covers how successful executives use intuitive expertise in acquisition decision-making, an important financial and strategic investment. This book also discusses the downsides of intuitive expertise such as biases and flawed decision-making. In sum, it provides a theoretical and empirically based ground for the topic. The content of the next five chapters is provided below:

Chapter 2—Experts and expertise: The chapter provides the reader with an overview of research on experts and expertise. Important constructs are defined and discussed. The limits of expertise are examined, for example, to what extent it is domain specific. The importance of innate abilities versus how deliberate practice affects the development of expertise is explained and related to neural mechanisms and pattern recognition.

Chapter 3—Intuition: The chapter starts by defining intuition based on research from the field of management. It is followed by an overview of research on dual-process theories, which describe and help us understand how we make judgments and decisions. These processes can be directly linked to intuitive decision-making. The chapter also covers how intuition can lead to flawed decisions.

Chapter 4—Intuitive expertise: In this chapter, intuitive expertise is introduced and defined, building on insights from the former chapters on expertise and intuition, respectively. The model presented in Chapter 1 will be further elaborated by explaining commonalities and differences between expertise and intuition. A third concept—intuitive expertise— is introduced and defined by its relation to the other two. The chapter ends with an overview of empirical studies of intuitive expertise.

Chapter 5—The empirical study: The findings from interviews of 12 high-performing senior executives are presented in this chapter. All of the executives have more than 20 years of experience in senior positions. Based on the interviews and insights from earlier studies, we are able to present findings that have practical and theoretical significance. Examples of these findings are: the characteristics, development, and use of intuitive expertise; areas of expertise; and the articulation of intuition.

Chapter 6—Conclusions: The last chapter summarizes the book and presents an analytical model. The findings from the analysis of earlier field studies and the new empirical study are discussed. We present implications for scholars and suggestions for future research. The chapter also includes suggestions for practitioners regarding how to nurture expertise and use intuition in financial decision-making.

Notes

1 The details of the empirical interview study, i.e., the methods used, are described in Appendix A. The interviewees are described in Appendix B.
2 Sometimes, the term "expert intuition" is used in the literature.

References

Akinci, C., & Sadler-Smith, E. (2012). Intuition in management research: A historical review. *International Journal of Management Reviews, 14*(1), 104–122.

APA (2021). Available at: https://dictionary.apa.org/ Accessed October 27, 2021.

Carlsen, M. (2020). *Skavlan*, SVT (Sveriges Television), February 7, 2020, 21.00–22.00 hrs.

Chase, W. G., & Simon, H. A. (1973). Perception in chess. *Cognitive psychology, 4*(1), 55–81.

Dane, E., & Pratt, M. G. (2007). Exploring intuition and its role in managerial decision making. *Academy of Management Review, 32*(1), 33–54.

De Groot, A. D. (1978). *Thought and choice in chess* (2nd ed.) (first Dutch edition in 1946). The Hague: Mouton Publishers.

Ericsson, K. A., Charness, N., Hoffman, R. R., & Feltovich, P. J. (Eds.). (2006). *The Cambridge handbook of expertise and expert performance.* New York, NY: Cambridge University Press.

Grant, M. (2018). *Making acquisitions.* Ph.D. Dissertation. Department of Business Studies, Uppsala University.

Grant, M., & Nilsson, F. (2020). The production of strategic and financial rationales in capital investments: Judgments based on intuitive expertise. *The British Accounting Review, 52*(3), 100861.

Grant, M., Nilsson, F., & Nordvall, A. C. (2020). The use of intuitive expertise in acquisition-making: An explorative study. In Sinclair, M. (Ed.). *Handbook of Intuition Research as Practice* (pp. 39–55). Cheltenham: Edward Elgar Publishing.

Hodgkinson, G. P., Langan-Fox, J., & Sadler-Smith, E. (2008). Intuition: A fundamental bridging construct in the behavioural sciences. *British Journal of Psychology, 99*(1), 1–27.

Koller, T., Goedhart, M., & Wessels, D. (2015). *Valuation: Measuring and managing the value of companies.* Hoboken, NJ: Wiley.

Kahneman, D., & Klein, G. (2009). Conditions for intuitive expertise: A failure to disagree. *American Psychologist, 64*(6), 515–526.

Mauboussin, M. J., Callahan, D., & Majd, D. (2016). Capital allocation: Evidence, analytical methods, and assessment guidance. *Credit Suisse,* October 19, 2016. Available at: https://research-doc.credit-suisse.com/ Accessed: October 27, 2021.

Mintzberg, H. (2000). *The rise and fall of strategic planning.* London: Prentice Hall, Financial Times.

Mintzberg, H., Raisinghani, D., & Théorêt, A. (1976). The structure of "unstructured" decision processes. *Administrative Science Quarterly, 21*(2), 246–275.

Polanyi, M. (2009). *The tacit dimension.* Chicago, IL: The University of Chicago Press. Originally published in 1966.

Salas, E., Rosen, M. A., & DiazGranados, D. (2010). Expertise-based intuition and decision making in organizations. *Journal of Management, 36*(4), 941–973.

Simon, H. A. (1992). What is an "explanation" of behavior? *Psychological Science, 3*(3), 150–161.

Sinclair, M. (Ed.). (2011). *Handbook of intuition research.* Cheltenham: Edward Elgar Publishing.

Tsoukas, H. (2003). Do we really understand tacit knowledge? In Easterby-Smith, M., & Lyles, M. A. (Eds.). *The Blackwell Handbook of Organizational Learning and Knowledge Management* (pp. 410–427). Oxford: Blackwell Publishing Ltd.

Ward, P., Schraagen, J. M., Gore, J., & Roth, E. M. (Eds.). (2020). *The Oxford handbook of expertise.* Oxford: Oxford University Press.

2 Experts and expertise

This chapter provides an overview of research on experts and expertise. The chapter has three main conclusions. First, an expert shows highly superior performance, consistently over a long period of time, within a specific domain and its related tasks. A domain is often similar to a profession, for example, a university professor, a CFO, or other senior executives. Second, the acquisition of expertise requires a long period of deliberate practice, typically 10 years or more. Pursuing such practice is highly demanding and requires motivation and persistence. Staying an expert is an everyday challenge with the overall objective to maintain and develop expert knowledge. Third, the effects of deliberate practice are supported by neural research. It shows that effects on the size and function of the brain are associated with the tasks related to expertise. Moreover, research shows that experts and novices cognitively "see" things differently, affecting how they store and recall experiences.

2.1 Defining expertise

The *Oxford English Dictionary* (OED, 2021) defines an "expert" as: (a) "A person who is expert or has gained skills from experience." (b) "A person regarded or consulted as an authority on account of special skill, training, or knowledge; a specialist." Expertise (a noun) is:

(a) Expert opinion or knowledge, often obtained through the action of submitting a matter to, and its consideration by, experts; an expert's appraisal, valuation, or report. (b) The quality or state of being expert; skill or expertness in a particular branch of study or sport.

DOI: 10.4324/9781003035725-2

Based on these definitions, we can discern two research perspectives: one psychological and one sociological. The psychological perspective studies expertise from an individual level of analysis without considering the social context. It defines expertise based on individual performance. In contrast, the sociological perspective is concerned with the social context of experts and expertise. One implication of this perspective is that expertise and being an expert are constructs that are not defined in absolute but in relative terms. For example, being an expert can be seen in relation to a layperson or alternatively to a more experienced and knowledgeable person. Moreover, research with a sociological perspective studies how expertise can render individuals prestige, privileges, and power stemming from their ability to exclude others who are not considered experts.

Two constructs closely linked to experts and expertise are professionals and professions. Both have attracted a great deal of interest in the field of sociology (Abbott, 1988). Belonging to a profession and being a professional—such as a lawyer, a doctor, or a certified public accountant (an auditor)—is often seen as being an expert in the view of a layperson. However, in fact, not all professionals are "true" experts in the sense of showing superior performance within their profession. If we take the example of a certified public accountant, there are several criteria to be met in order to be approved and awarded the title. For example, in Sweden, this includes having a university-level education encompassing certain subject areas, logging several years of practice at an auditing firm, and passing a written exam. However, as is the case with other professionals like specialist doctors, being a certified public accountant does not mean that you necessarily perform at a high or outstanding level. Research has shown that other characteristics, such as appearance and behavior, could play a more important role than performance does in being a professional (Grey, 1998). Hence, not all professionals are experts. To be an expert requires expertise that is clearly visible in a high or a superior performance in a specific domain.

In this book, we will focus on expertise and individual performance. We will, therefore, draw on research in expertise and expert performance from the field of psychology. Even though the field is mature, the first handbook of expertise and expert performance was published by Ericsson et al. as recently as 2006.[1] Following this line of research, an important theoretical starting point for us is Ericsson and Smith (1991), which outlined a general theory and definition of expertise. As summarized by Ericsson and Lehman (1996, p. 277), this definition can be described as "consistently superior performance on a specified set of representative tasks for a domain." This definition was developed together with a framework for the study of expertise, built on the seminal works of chess by De Groot (1946/1978) and Chase and Simon (1973a, 1973b; Simon & Chase, 1973).

De Groot (1946/1978) was interested in the underlying thought processes of chess players, and especially those who were characterized as chess masters. The method he used was to let them think aloud when selecting the next move. He found, in contrast to the general idea at that time, that chess masters did not think further ahead, using longer move combinations than those less skilled. Instead, it seemed that chess masters had superior memory for chess positions and relied on patterns stored in their memory.

Chase and Simon (1973a, 1973b; Simon & Chase, 1973) developed this further and argued that it was not possible to find mechanisms such as a general memory span that measures chess skill. They stated that "chess skill depends in large part upon a vast, organized long-term memory of specific information about chessboard patterns" and hence "the overriding factor in chess skill is practice" (Chase & Simon, 1973b, pp. 492–493).

Returning to the definition of expertise by Ericsson and Smith (1991), their delineation was developed together with a conceptual framework for the scientific inquiry "to understand and account for what distinguishes outstanding individuals in a domain from less outstanding individuals in that domain, as well as from people in general" (1991, p. 2). Drawing on the works of De Groot (1946/1978) and Chase and Simon (1973a, 1973b; Simon & Chase, 1973), they identified three steps of the inquiry.

First, the inquiry should cover a set of representative tasks that captures superior performance in a specific domain. These tasks and the superior performance should be replicable in an experimental setting. Examples of domains for which the identification of representative tasks has been easy to find are chess, memory sport, mental calculators, typing, and some sports. However, in other more complex real-life situations, defining representative tasks is much more difficult. For example, can a medical diagnosis be represented in an experiment with written cases and will it reflect interviews and meetings with real patients? Furthermore, outstanding performance is related to stable characteristics possessed by the expert. In an experiment, it is therefore necessary to be able to replicate performance and to have a control group to compare with. This rules out single achievements in unique situations, for example, the achievements of heads of state or people with large economic resources.

Second, the inquiry should include a comprehensive examination of superior performance "to infer the underlying cognitive processes mediating superior performance, as well as the use of experimental manipulation of stimulus materials" (Ericsson & Smith, 1991, p. 12). In this step, methods of cognitive science are used to elicit mediating cognitive structures and processes. Examples are studies of reaction time, eye fixation, keystrokes (typing), and think-aloud protocols.

Third, theories and empirical data are used to explain how the identified mediating structures and processes can be acquired through learning and adaption. Chase and Simon (1973b) single out past experience as especially important, arguing that a typical chess master's elaborate range of chessboard patterns, organized in the long-term memory (LTM), requires thousands of hours to acquire.

To summarize, the definition of expertise by Ericsson and Smith (1991) has its roots in a scientific methodology that is based on replicability and experimental studies. Hence, it is based on the performance of standardized tasks where superior performance can be demonstrated. It also necessitates that the mediating processes can be identified. However, it is not always possible to fulfill these requirements. Furthermore, many professional positions require skills in several areas, which is not the case when playing chess. For example, a university professor should excel in research and teaching, including such diverse skills as writing, pedagogics, and administration. Another example is professional positions in the field of accounting, such as CFOs, controllers, or certified public accountants. These positions require a wide variety of skills across a multitude of tasks. Therefore, representative tasks that lend themselves to replicability and experiments are hard, if not even impossible, to find in these domains. To be able to study financial decision-making, it is thus necessary to apply a definition suited to this area of expertise and also use a somewhat different scientific methodology than that suggested by Ericsson and Smith (1991).

More relaxed criteria for studying expertise have been suggested by Gobet (2016) and others (e.g., Dreyfus & Dreyfus, 1986; Hoffman, 1998, 2019; Weiss & Shanteau, 2014). These criteria are well suited for examining the expertise of professionals such as CFOs or university professors. Gobet (2016, p. 5) defines an expert as "somebody who obtains results that are vastly superior to those obtained by the majority of the population." This adds another layer to the definition of an expert, a so-called "super-expert somebody whose performance is vastly superior to the majority of experts" (ibid., p. 5).

There are also authors emphasizing that the development of expertise should be seen as steps along a continuum rather than a dichotomy between experts and non-experts. For example, Dreyfus and Dreyfus (1986) present a model of skill acquisition consisting of five stages: novice, advanced beginner, competence, proficiency, and expertise. The first three steps involve a detached and deliberate form of making judgments, largely resembling analytical thinking. The stages of proficiency and expertise are characterized by what the authors call "holistic discrimination and association," that is, "the ability to intuitively respond to patterns without decomposing them into component features" (Dreyfus & Dreyfus, 1986, p. 28). In a similar manner, Hoffman (1998, p. 85) draws a parallel to the classifications of craft guilds in the Middle Ages. In these guilds, an expert is described as:

> *The distinguished or brilliant journeyman, highly regarded by peers, whose judgments are uncommonly accurate and reliable, whose performance shows consummate skill and economy of effort, and who can deal effectively with certain types of rare or "tough" cases. Also, an expert is one who has special skills or knowledge derived from extensive experience with subdomains.*

Later, Hoffman (2019, p. 3) uses this description to illustrate methods that can be used to identify an expert. Examples of methods mentioned by him are in-depth interviews about education, training, etc. and asking about professional achievements.

We adhere to these more relaxed definitions and views of expertise as a continuum. They allow us to analyze experts and expertise in domains related to financial decision-making, that is, high-performing senior executives. These decision-makers do not fully lend themselves to the type of study that fulfills the requirements of Ericsson and Smith (1991). However, when evaluating performance, we will apply a long time-perspective in line with Ericsson's emphasis on consistency. A reason for this is the existence of chance and risk, which can significantly affect short-term performance.

2.2 Expertise is domain and task dependent

Expertise is related to a domain and specific tasks within that domain. For example, an expert classical piano player has different expertise and skills than a violinist. A grand master chess player has a different set of expertise and skills than an expert bridge player. Depending on the characteristics of the tasks, a domain can be more or less prone to expertise. In some domains, expert performance can even be difficult to observe at all. Examples of these domains are economic and political forecasts, especially if they cover long-term effects (e.g., Kay & King, 2020). Another example is making a prognosis of technological development and the future success of new technologies in the marketplace. An often-quoted example of how difficult this can be is from Steve Ballmer in 2007, at that time the CEO of Microsoft, commenting on the future of the iPhone. He stated that "[t]here is no chance that the iPhone is going to get any significant market share. No chance." (Tetlock & Gardner, 2015, p. 46)

Domains can be narrow and encompass a few tasks or broader encompassing a range of tasks. The example of a narrow domain, mentioned earlier, is chess, which early on provided seminal research on expertise (Chase & Simon, 1973a, 1973b; De Groot 1946/1978; Simon & Chase, 1973; see also Gobet & Charness, 2006). In sports (Hodges et al., 2006) and music (Ericsson et al., 1993), domains are also typically narrow.

There are also broader domains consisting of several tasks, which can be characterized as ill structured. An example of this is the research field of history, which has unstructured problems with different solutions and hence lacks right-or-wrong answers. In this domain, expertise can be analyzed based on the tasks of obtaining information, making a narrative construction and analysis, and reasoning and problem solving (Voss & Wiley, 2006). Another example with similar characteristics is professional writing, a poorly structured task with numerous goals (Kellogg, 2006). It can be seen as encompassing a single domain or as several domains requiring a variety of skills. Novelists, poets, screen writers, scientists, and journalists are examples of professional writers. Their skills do not necessarily overlap, and a poet is likely to be a rather poor scientific writer. However, there are still some features that seem to apply to all of them, such as extensive reading in their genre and domain, high verbal ability, and use of concrete language (Kellogg, 2006).

The previous examples of university professors, CFOs, and other corporate decision-makers can be described as working over broad, perhaps even multiple domains. Still, the tasks of judgments can be seen as vital across these and many other professions (Weiss & Shanteau, 2014). For example, in the fields of accounting and finance, CFOs and other decision-makers make judgments about companies they have or want to acquire, all impacting the future development and value of the company. Furthermore, judgments are commonplace when making decisions to employ someone or assessing the performance of employees. For a university professor, judgments are also frequent. Examples are when selecting PhD candidates, or when assessing manuscripts or a thesis.

Even experts can, obviously, show poor performance. One example is when environmental factors unexpectedly change, or random events occur, affecting the financial markets (Kay & King, 2020; Taleb, 2007). Hence, it is consistency and performance seen over a longer period of time that characterizes experts and expertise in a domain (Ericsson & Smith, 1991). However, there are domains for which expertise is difficult or almost impossible to attain. An example is long-term economic forecasts, where a myriad of factors and events can influence the outcome. An economist expressed the randomness of the outcome as "the unexpected usually occurs, as it can happen in an infinite number of ways while the expected rarely occurs, since it can only happen in one way" (Lindbeck, 2012, p. 387, translated by the authors). At the other end of the spectrum, we have domains in which expertise and consistently superior performance is achievable. Kahneman and Klein (2009, p. 520) refer to these domains as low- or high-validity environments, meaning that "the causal and statistical structure of the relevant environment" is weak or strong.

In a more detailed manner, Shanteau (1992) analyzed research findings on expertise in different domains and suggested that the task characteristics of a domain are a determining factor of expertise performance. In the paper, he listed domains for which, respectively, strong and weak performance had been found. Examples of domains in which strong expert performance had been found were weather forecasters, mathematicians, and accountants. In contrast, studies of court judges, recruiters, intelligence analysts, and stockbrokers showed weak performance. In some domains, such as nurses, and auditors, both strong and weak performance had been found. These domains showed expertise in some of their tasks but not in all. An example is that auditors can be experts in managing hard data but do less well in assessing soft data and fraud (Kahneman & Klein, 2009).

Based on the performance of experts from different domains, Shanteau (1992) identified task characteristics related to performance. In a later article, Shanteau (2015) developed this further and identified domain characteristics that seem to affect whether the domain lends itself to expertise or not (see Table 2.1). In this work, he also solicited and received comments from key scholars in the field such as Dawes, Edwards, Gigerenzer, Hammond, and Klein.

Table 2.1 Task characteristics (Adapted from Shanteau, 2015, p. 172)

Characteristic	Good performance	Poor performance
1 Stimulus stability	Static	Dynamic
2 Type of decision	Physical system	Behavioral system
3 Experts agree on cues?	Yes	No
4 Domain context	Predictable	Unpredictable
5 Errors in decision-making	Tolerated	Not tolerated
6 Repetitive tasks?	Yes	No
7 Outcome feedback?	Available	Unavailable
8 Problem decomposition?	Yes	No
9 Use of decision aids?	Routine	Not routine

Table 2.1 is based on empirical research from that time, although much of it was carried out in the 1960s and 1970s. The column "Good performance" provides characteristics of stable or predictive tasks, where people have the opportunity to learn. The column "Poor performance" covers tasks that are difficult to learn since they are greatly affected by dynamics and randomness. The characteristics found in the table should be regarded as suggestions. Thus, the columns good performance and poor performance should not be viewed as something absolute but rather as a continuum.

The first four characteristics are related to the predictability of the task and the context. Shanteau and other researchers (e.g., Thomas & Lawrence, 2018) argue that especially human behavior is typically difficult to predict. Examples they present to support this claim, such as predicting whether a person will relapse into criminal behavior, are taken from clinical psychology. In contrast to this, a physical system like the weather and how it is going to develop can be predicted in the short term, even though it is very complex to do so.

The following three characteristics are related to whether errors are tolerated in decision-making, repetition, and feedback. These are vital for learning and tie into the concept of deliberate practice described in the following section. An example of an area with poor feedback is clinical psychology, as feedback is slow, if it is provided at all (Thomas & Lawrence, 2018). In contrast, the area of accounting and finance is characterized by repetition and feedback, with regular reporting and follow-up as vital tasks.

The last two characteristics relate to the structure of tasks and access to decision aids. In many domains, models and tools have been developed that can support judgments and decisions. Consequently, when models, tools, and knowledge are developed, a domain can change from poor to good performance. It is moving in the direction of becoming a domain benign for expertise. Examples of models and tools that have made domains more benign for expertise are weather models for meteorologists, MRI (Magnetic Resonance Image) scans for medical diagnosticians, and support tools and models for geologists (Thomas & Lawrence, 2018).

Recent research argues that adaptability is an essential part of expertise (Ward et al., 2018, 2020). Adaptability is related to an individual's skilled adaption to change. An example is the ability to use knowledge in changing contexts, and hence to deal with change. Furthermore, adaptability includes expertise in cases occurring with a low frequency. This suggests that changing domain contexts and lower frequency tasks are not necessarily characterizations of domains with poor performance, but rather that the ability to deal with these is a characteristic of expertise.

The dynamic aspect of domains and tasks is, to some extent, found in most of the characteristics in Table 2.1. As domains and tasks become more mature—for example through advances in our knowledge, and the models and tools used—they can move from poor to good performance, rendering them ripe for expertise. Division of work and increasing specialization can arguably also advance our knowledge in some domains. Furthermore, dynamic aspects driven by decision aids, and specifically IT systems, including machine learning, are especially relevant in today's environment (Ågerfalk, 2020). For example, in the financial sector, new investment themes can be developed based on the availability of and capacity to process large amounts of data (Dimson et al., 2018), perhaps making the domain more prone to the development of expertise.

2.3 Becoming an expert

How people acquire expertise and become experts in a domain depends not only on the length and quality of practice but also on genetic and environmental factors. Researchers interested in the quality of practice have, to a great extent, been influenced by the concept of deliberate practice, developed by Ericsson et al. (1993). They showed that a necessary requirement for being able to improve performance in a domain is a long period of high-quality practice. Such deliberate practice is defined as "activities invented with the primary purpose of attaining and improving skills" (Ericsson et al., 1993, p. 367). These activities must be adapted to the needs of the individual, consider pre-existing knowledge, and challenge and push the individual outside their comfort zone. Furthermore, deliberate practice should include immediate, actionable feedback and repetition. By performing the same, or similar, tasks repeatedly and getting feedback, successive refinement will be facilitated. A final characteristic is that deliberate practice requires that the person be well motivated and possess strong perseverance. The reason is that long periods of demanding training, with full concentration, are an essential component of deliberate practice. This, however, is not always enjoyable.

Ericsson et al. (1993) claimed that deliberate practice constitutes the determining factor of developing expertise. Following this early publication by Ericsson et al. (1993), a large number of studies have been carried out that examine deliberate practice and its role in developing expertise (Hambrick et al., 2016). These also encompass studies by researchers from fields such as genetics and neuroscience (Hambrick et al., 2016; Plomin et al., 2014; Ullén et al., 2016). Findings from these studies show that genetic and environmental factors can also play a large role, re-sparking the perennial debate about nature (genetics) versus nurture (environmental factors, including deliberate practice) in the development of expertise (Ericsson, 2021; Hambrick et al., 2016; Miller et al., 2020; Ullén et al., 2016).

The section below contains a short overview of the current knowledge of how genetic and environmental factors influence the development of expertise. This overview is followed by two sections relating that knowledge to research on deliberate practice.

2.3.1 Genetic and environmental influence

Genetic and environmental factors are difficult to separate. However, genetic influence has been shown to influence expertise. In a large meta-analysis, encompassing 2,748 publications published between 1958 and 2012, Polderman et al. (2015) concluded that all human traits are heritable, since they did not find any traits with an estimated weighted heritability[2] of zero. Arguably, human traits such as temperament, personality, and higher-level cognitive functions affect how we acquire expertise. Thus, it seems rather evident that there is a heritable element in expertise. For example, physical traits are strongly influenced by genetic factors,[3] and it is self-evident that in basketball, to take an example from the field of sports, height is important. Similarly, the shape and size of the hand and fingers can affect piano skills (Ullén et al., 2016). These two examples show that heritable traits can affect, to some degree, the level of expertise in a specific field.

There is also evidence that psychological traits (e.g., personality, ability, and motivation) and environmental factors influence the acquisition of expertise. Heritability typically accounts for between 30% and 60% of psychological traits (Plomin et al., 2014). For example, Plomin et al. (2014) studied reading performance by 12-year-old twins. At this age, life-long reading performance is established. The study showed that heritance was the major explanatory factor for the difference in performance between experts and normal readers, explaining more than half of the difference. Environmental factors such as the schools they attended explained less than a fifth of the difference in performance.

Another example, related to the discussion of psychological traits, is grit, which can be defined as a "passion for and perseverance toward especially long-term goals" (Duckworth & Gross, 2014, p. 319). Grit is related to motivation and has been shown to be associated with educational achievements and professional success. The importance of endurance and motivation can also be seen in studies of children. For example, Winner (2000, p. 162) argues in her work on gifted children that, apart from innate abilities, these children "have a deep intrinsic motivation to master the domain in which they have their high ability and are almost maniac in their energy level." A study by Mosing et al. (2016) provides a similar argument, that is, that an individual with an inherent trait, for example, high intelligence, is more likely to persist in practicing and learning to master a domain. Hence, a psychological trait such as grit, which is partly inherited, is one explanation why people differ in their propensity to engage and persist in practicing and learning skills within a domain.

2.3.2 Length of practice

It is well established that it takes a long time of deliberate practice to acquire expertise in a specific domain. Simon and Chase (1973, p. 402) identified this as the most important factor in developing skills in playing chess. They could not find any case "where a person has reached grandmaster level with less than about a decade's intense preoccupation with the game. We would estimate, very roughly, that a master has spent perhaps 10,000 to 50,000 hours staring at chess positions." This finding received support from Ericsson et al. (1993, p. 366) in their paper on deliberate practice. They named it the Simon and Chase "10-year rule" by providing support for it from other studies of music, mathematics, swimming, and long-distance running. However, they also added some nuances to the rule by providing examples of studies where longer periods had been observed. One example is musical composition, which often requires more than 20 years of practice before a first outstanding piece is composed.

In fact, studies show that there are large variations across domains regarding the amount of practice that is required to become an expert (Ericsson & Ward, 2007; Ericsson et al., 1993; Hambrick et al., 2016). For example, in his early career, Ericsson conducted a memory experiment with a highly motivated participant, Steve, to understand how numbers could be remembered and recalled. After about 230 hours of training sessions Steve could remember and recall almost 80 digits (Ericsson et al., 1980). It should be noted, however, that studies show that there are significant individual differences in the amount of practice required to become an expert, even in the same domain (e.g., Ericsson et al., 1993; Gobet & Ereku, 2014; Hambrick et al., 2016).

How much time is required to reach a high level of expertise is also dependent on when practice is started. It seems like some abilities are easier to practice and develop in certain age spans. One example is having a perfect pitch in music, which seems to be advantageous to learn between 3 and 5 years of age (Ericsson & Ward, 2007). Furthermore, expertise needs to be developed and maintained by continuing high-quality practice (Krampe & Charness, 2006). For example, and as described in the previous section on domain and task dependence, an expert needs to be updated on new methods and aids in the domain.

2.3.3 The debate on nature and nurture

Based on a review of studies in the field of expertise, Ericsson et al. (1993) concluded that heritable characteristics could not explain expert performance. The only exceptions to that conclusion were certain physical attributes, such as height, which could affect performance in sports. Moreover, they found a weak to moderate positive association between the amount of practice and the performance achieved. Consequently, they argued that practice and its quality needed to be analyzed in more detail to better understand how expertise is developed.

Based on studies of learning and skill acquisition, they concluded that conditions for effective training, that is, leading to large improvements in performance, include motivation, feedback, and repetition. They wrote (ibid., p. 367):

> *The most cited condition concerns the subjects' motivation to attend to the task and exert effort to improve their performance. In addition, the design of the task should take into account the pre-existing knowledge of the learners so that the task can be correctly understood after a brief period of instruction. The subjects should receive immediate*

informative feedback and knowledge of results of their performance. The subjects should repeatedly perform the same or similar tasks.

Based on these findings, and their own study of violinists and pianists, Ericsson et al. (1993, p. 400) argued that "We view elite performance as the product of a decade or more of maximal efforts to improve performance in a domain through an optimal distribution of deliberate practice." Thus, even though Ericsson et al. (1993) did not rule out the influence of environmental factors and innate abilities—what we in everyday speech call "talent"—they argued that most of what we can observe as elite performance can be explained by deliberate practice.[4]

That deliberate practice is the most important independent variable when explaining variance in elite performance is a position that Ericsson and others have largely stayed with since the seminal paper of 1993 (e.g., Ericsson, 2006b, 2021; Ericsson & Harwell, 2019; Keith & Ericsson, 2007). They have done so despite the existence of findings showing that genetics and environmental factors influence the development of expertise, as shown in the previous section. Moreover, meta-analysis of some of the research on the relationship between deliberate practice and expertise has questioned whether the former is the major explanatory variable for superior performance (Macnamara et al., 2014; 2016). As mentioned above, questioning this fundamental relationship has reignited the old debate about nature versus nurture.

A key argument in the critique has been that some studies and meta-analyses show that deliberate practice does not account for the majority of the variance in performance. Still, these studies and analysis support the importance of deliberate practice in explaining performance differences (Hambrick et al., 2016; Macnamara, 2016; Miller et al., 2020). As an example, Miller et al. (2020) performed a re-analysis of the meta-analysis by Macnamara et al. (2014) and found that the correlation coefficient for the deliberate practice effect was 0.40. That is almost twice as high as the correlation for practice that did not qualify as deliberate practice. Moreover, Miller et al. (2020) put these coefficients in context by comparing them with corresponding numbers from studies of factors affecting health and mortality, such as obesity (0.08), excessive drinking (0.13), or smoking (0.21). They argue that these correlations are seldom questioned, and a few would argue, based on this scientific evidence, that excessive drinking or smoking is not bad for one's health. Hence, a correlation coefficient of 0.40 cannot be ignored or claimed to be low by any measure.

2.4 Neural and memory mechanisms

We have, so far, placed a lot of emphasis on the importance of deliberate practice to become an expert. In this section, we add to that discussion by presenting two underlying mechanisms that can contribute toward increasing our understanding of expertise across different domains. First, research has shown that deliberate practice in sports, music, mathematics, and other domains affects the function and structure of the brain, so-called neural mechanisms, in a way that facilitates the development of expertise. Second, research has also shown that what a novice or an expert perceptually "sees" and remembers differs. These findings provide insights into how a novice and an expert reason and the importance of memory mechanisms when expertise is developed.

2.4.1 Neural mechanisms of expertise

Studies show that deliberate practice can lead to a change in the structure and function of the brain. All in all, the results suggest that these changes are one explanation, among others, of how expertise develops. Let us, therefore, take a closer look at some of the results starting with an early study of London taxi drivers.

London taxi drivers spend 3–4 years of training to master what is labeled "the Knowledge," that is, knowing how to find any street, road, or place in London where a passenger can ask to be taken. This includes thousands of streets and places. Subsequent stringent assessments, including an examination process in six stages, need to be passed in order to get a license. The results from the study of this massive training exercise showed an increase in tissue volume in a part of the brain associated with spatial memory and navigation (Maguire et al., 2000). The researchers suggest "that the 'mental map' of the city is stored in the posterior hippocampus and is accommodated by an increase in tissue volume" (ibid., p. 4402).

Another example is a study by Draganski et al. (2004) on how training juggling affects the brain. Juggling is a complex motor skill requiring coordinated arm movements, grasping, and visual tracking. Two groups, jugglers and a control group were set up. The jugglers had 3 months to learn three-ball cascade juggling, sustaining juggling for at least 60 seconds. The following 3 months, the jugglers did not practice the skill, and most subjects lost their ability to juggle. The findings show that training induced changes in brain areas related to the ability to integrate visual perception and movement of the body, that is, visuo-motor skills. Furthermore, 3 months after the exercise had ended, the increase in the affected brain areas decreased.

The effect on the brain by practicing juggling was followed up with a study by Scholz et al. (2009), which examined changes in brain tissue and nerve tracts.[5] Their findings showed changes in the brain tissue associated with visuo-motor skills and changes in nerve tracts. Consequently, they concluded that training induces changes in the amount of nerve cells and nerve tracts, affecting the structure and function of the brain.

Studies of experts in the domain of music, including musical improvisation (Pinho et al., 2014) and mathematics (Jeon et al., 2019), show similar effects on the brain. Other similar examples can be found in the domains of professional simultaneous interpreters, perfumers, and athletes (Ullén et al., 2016). Taken together, these and other studies strongly suggest that changes in the brain caused by deliberate training are an important explanation for the development of expertise. Perhaps somewhat speculatively, changes in the structure and function of the brain shown in these studies might reflect the general mechanisms applicable in other domains, such as university professors or CFOs. Similar thoughts have been put forward by Jeon et al. (2019), who suggested their findings on mathematical expertise could possibly reflect "a general principle of cognitive expertise" (Jeon et al, 2019, p. 1).

2.4.2 *What experts and novices "see" and remember*

The role of memory and what we perceptually "see" and store in our short-term memory (STM) and LTM is a vital mechanism for developing expertise. Many of the findings in this research area emanate from the seminal works on the study of chess by De Groot (1946/1978) and Chase and Simon (1973a, 1973b; Simon & Chase, 1973).

De Groot's dissertation (1946/1978) analyzed chess players' thinking as they talked aloud while planning a move. As we pointed out in an earlier section, he found that chess masters did not think differently than less skilled players. For example, they did not search differently, in terms of number of moves, depth of search (moves ahead), or speed of search. Still, chess masters found the best move, and it was found within the first few seconds. In another experiment, he studied a recall task. Chess players were shown a chess board for 2–10 seconds, and they were then asked to reconstruct this from memory. The findings showed major differences between masters and grand masters (approximately 93% correct) and good amateurs (about 33%).

Chase and Simon (1973a) examined what chess players, especially experienced players, "see," that is, what they perceive when they look at chess positions. The premise was that STM has a very limited capacity and that there is no difference between masters and other players (around seven items can be stored). With that starting point, they reasoned that the high performance by masters could possibly be explained by how they perceive structures, that is, what they "see" and how that is represented in STM, or in their own words: "Our main concern here is to discover and characterize the structures, or chunks, that are seen on the board and stored in short-term memory" (ibid., p. 56). In their study, they used two methods: first, a perceptual task where players looked at a chessboard and replicated it at the same time; second, a memory task where players first saw a chessboard and then replicated it. The idea was that if only a short time-period is provided to complete the task, only STM can be used. The conclusion from their study was that superior performance "derives from the ability of those players to encode the position into larger perceptual chunks, each consisting of a familiar subconfiguration of pieces." (ibid., p. 80)

In subsequent papers, Simon and Chase (Chase & Simon, 1973b; Simon & Chase, 1973) summarized their findings into what has been labeled *the chunking theory.* As the name suggests, a key element is that information about chessboard positions is coded in chunks that are meaningful to the player. In that way, information can be stored and re-trieved more efficiently from STM and LTM, in comparison to storing each individual chess piece. Their research also shows that long-time practice builds up a vast number of chessboard patterns in LTM. Fur-thermore, Simon and Chase suggested mechanisms of how the inter-play could work between what they saw as limited information capacity in the STM and the retrieval of information from the LTM.

Later research has shown that the chunking theory overemphasizes the role of STM. For example, in recall tasks, LTM can also be used. This claim is based on findings suggesting that storage and retrieval of information in LTM is faster than the chunking theory assumes. Based on these findings, other theories have been suggested (Gobet, 2016, 2020) even though they mostly build on the works of Chase and Simon. It should be pointed out, however, that there is substantial ev-idence for chunking as an information-processing mechanism. Gobet et al. (2001) divides chunking into deliberate, conscious chunking and more automatic, perceptual chunking. An example of deliberate chunking is the previously mentioned memory experiment by Erics-son et al. (1980) in which the participant, Steve, who was a runner, connected, or encoded, random digits to larger chunks of running times of different races. Arguably, most of the chunking is automatic and takes place continuously during perception (Gobet et al., 2001).

Chunking mechanisms in learning are supported not only by research on memory tests and chess but also in domains such as verbal learning and concept formation (ibid.). A salient example of this is how letters are grouped into words, sentences, and paragraphs.

Moreover, there is a strong relationship between the level of expertise and how we remember meaningful information. Hence, what we store in memory, the chunks and how we retrieve information, is important. For example, a study of how experts and novices represent and categorize problems in physics shows that experts take a longer time to sort or categorize problems than novices (Chi et al., 1981). However, what they "see" is different. Novices see what the authors name "surface structures," such as visual similarities or key words, and they use them to sort the problems into categories. Experts' representation of the problems or what they "see" are "deep structures," in this case the major principles of physics governing the solution. An alternative way to phrase it is to say that experts and novices have different knowledge structures, that is, "schemas." Another example of memory for meaningful information by experts is football, where the recognition of perceptual patterns helps players anticipate the move of their opponents and their own players and plan for future action based on that (Ward & Williams, 2003). Similar findings can be seen in studies of games (such as chess, go, and bridge), programming, and music (Gobet, 2016).

To conclude, at a general level, expertise is arguably about what we perceptually "see" and what we store in memory. Research has pointed to different explanations for how these patterns, or chunks, are formed, stored, and recalled from memory. Novices and experts "see" different things, and they reason differently. Examples of differences are that experts take more time to understand problems conceptually and have richer conceptual representations. Furthermore, experts are flexible in their reasoning and are able to generate scenarios or frameworks in new and novel situations (Hoffman, 1998; Klein, 2017). Thus, expertise is also about adapting to new situations. This is an ability that is highly valuable, not least in the changing business environment of today (Ward et al., 2018, 2020).

2.5 Summary

An expert can be seen as "somebody who obtains results that are vastly superior to those obtained by the majority of the population" (Gobet, 2016, p. 5). The result, or performance, should be seen along a continuum starting with being a novice. After many years of high-quality training—so-called deliberate practice—the novice can become an expert. An expert can be identified through, for example, assessments by peers, the breadth and depth of experience, and the criteria for what it takes to reach the top in a certain area.

Expertise is strongly related to a domain and the tasks carried out in that domain. For example, a classical piano player has different expertise and skills than a violinist. Domains can also be broad, encompassing several tasks such as those of a university professor, a CFO, or other senior executives. A critical task across these domains is judgments. Depending on their characteristics, domains and tasks can be more or less benign to expertise. For example, long-term economic forecasting is likely not prone to expertise as the outcome is influenced by too many variables, many of which are unknown. However, as knowledge and tools develop, the domain becomes more prone to expertise. An example is the development of IT systems, including machine learning.

A long period of deliberate practice is required to become an expert. However, this might not be enough, as genetics and environmental factors also play a role. Leaving that aside, the development of expertise is supported by conditions for improving performance, which include a long period of deliberate practice. This transition typically takes a decade or more of training in the specific area, where important elements are feedback and follow-up. The quest for expertise should also be challenging, stretching one's capacity, with successive refinement. In order to follow this regimen year after year, psychological traits such as grit, motivation, and perseverance are vital.

Neural and memory mechanisms are involved in deliberate practice and important for our understanding of expertise. Deliberate practice affects the regions and connections in the brain that are involved in the tasks. Memory mechanisms affect what we cognitively "see," remember, and recall. Novices and experts experience different things and reason differently. An example is that experts take more time to understand problems conceptually and "see deep structures"; they have richer conceptual representations. Novices, on the other hand, "see surface structures," such as visual similarities or key words. Furthermore, experts are flexible in their reasoning and can generate scenarios or frameworks in novel situations.

Notes

1 For a historical overview, see Ericsson (2006a).
2 Heritability is: "an effect size index of the proportion of phenotypic variance that is accounted for by genetic variance" Plomin et al. (2014, p. 46). Merriam Webster Dictionary defines phenotypic as: "the observable characteristics or traits of an organism that are produced by the

interaction of the genotype and the environment: the physical expression of one or more genes."
3 Anthropometric properties (body measures) typically have heritability in the range of 70% to 90% (Ullén et al., 2016).
4 It can be noted that Ericsson et al. (1993) and subsequent articles and books (e.g., Ericsson, 2006b, 2021; Ericsson & Lehman, 1996) do not define deliberate practice in a detailed manner, leaving it partly open for interpretation. A reason for this could be that deliberate practice varies across domains.
5 A bundle of nerve fibers connecting nerve cells.

References

Abbott, A. (1988). *The system of professions: An essay on the division of expert labor.* Chicago, IL: University of Chicago Press.

Ågerfalk, P. J. (2020). Artificial intelligence as digital agency. *European Journal of Information Systems, 29*(1), 1–8.

Chase, W. G., & Simon, H. A. (1973a). Perception in chess. *Cognitive Psychology, 4*(1), 55–81.

Chase, W. G., & Simon, H. A. (1973b). The mind's eye in chess. In Chase, W. G. (Ed.), *Visual Information Processing* (pp. 461–494). New York, NY: Academic Press.

Chi, M. T., Feltovich, P. J., & Glaser, R. (1981). Categorization and representation of physics problems by experts and novices. *Cognitive Science, 5*(2), 121–152.

De Groot, A. D. (1978). *Thought and choice in chess* (2nd ed.) (first Dutch edition in 1946). The Hague: Mouton Publishers.

Dimson, E., Marsh, P., & Staunton, M. (2018). Practical applications of factor-based investing: The long-term evidence. *Practical Applications, 5*(3), 1–5.

Draganski, B., Gaser, C., Busch, V., Schuierer, G., Bogdahn, U., & May, A. (2004). Changes in grey matter induced by training. *Nature, 427*(6972), 311–312.

Dreyfus, H. L., & Dreyfus, S. E. (1986). *Mind over machine – The power of human intuition and expertise in the era of the computer.* New York, NY: The Free Press.

Duckworth, A., & Gross, J. J. (2014). Self-control and grit: Related but separable determinants of success. *Current Directions in Psychological Science, 23*(5), 319–325.

Ericsson, K. A. (2006a). An introduction to the Cambridge handbook of expertise and expert performance: Its development, organization, and content. In Ericsson, K. A., Charness, N., Feltovich, P. J., & Hoffman, R. R. (Eds.). *The Cambridge Handbook of Expertise and Expert Performance* (pp. 3–19). New York, NY: Cambridge University Press.

Ericsson, K. A. (2006b). The influence of experience and deliberate practice on the development of superior expert performance. In Ericsson, K. A., Charness, N., Feltovich, P. J., & Hoffman, R. R. (Eds.). *The Cambridge handbook of expertise and expert performance* (pp. 683–703). New York: Cambridge University Press.

Ericsson, K. A. (2021). Given that the detailed original criteria for deliberate practice have not changed, could the understanding of this complex concept have improved over time? A response to Macnamara and Hambrick (2020). *Psychological Research, 85*(3), 1114–1120.

Ericsson, K. A., Charness, N., Hoffman, R. R., & Feltovich, P. J. (Eds.). (2006). *The Cambridge handbook of expertise and expert performance*. New York, NY: Cambridge University Press.

Ericsson, K. A., Chase, W. G., & Faloon, S. (1980). Acquisition of a memory skill. *Science, 208*(4448), 1181–1182.

Ericsson, K. A., & Harwell, K. W. (2019). Deliberate practice and proposed limits on the effects of practice on the acquisition of expert performance: Why the original definition matters and recommendations for future research. *Frontiers in Psychology, 10*, 2396.

Ericsson, K. A., Krampe, R. T., & Tesch-Römer, C. (1993). The role of deliberate practice in the acquisition of expert performance. *Psychological Review, 100*(3), 363–406.

Ericsson, K. A., & Lehmann, A. C. (1996). Expert and exceptional performance: Evidence of maximal adaptation to task constraints. *Annual Review of Psychology, 47*(1), 273–305.

Ericsson, K. A., & Smith, J. (1991). *Toward a general theory of expertise: Prospects and limits*. Cambridge: Cambridge University Press.

Ericsson, K. A., & Ward, P. (2007). Capturing the naturally occurring superior performance of experts in the laboratory: Toward a science of expert and exceptional performance. *Current Directions in Psychological Science, 16*(6), 346–350.

Gobet, F. (2016). *Understanding expertise: A multi-disciplinary approach*. London: Red Globe Press.

Gobet, F. (2020). The classic expertise approach and its evolution. In Ward, P., Schraagen, J. M., Gore, J., & Roth, E. (Eds.). *The Oxford Handbook of Expertise* (pp. 35–55). Oxford: Oxford University Press.

Gobet, F., & Charness, N. (2006). Expertise in chess. In Ericsson, K. A., Charness, N., Feltovich, P. J., & Hoffman, R. R., (Eds.). *The Cambridge Handbook of Expertise and Expert Performance* (pp. 523–538). New York, NY: Cambridge University Press.

Gobet, F., & Ereku, M. H. (2014). Checkmate to deliberate practice: The case of Magnus Carlsen. *Frontiers in Psychology, 5*(878), 1–3.

Gobet, F., Lane, P. C., Croker, S., Cheng, P. C., Jones, G., Oliver, I., & Pine, J. M. (2001). Chunking mechanisms in human learning. *Trends in Cognitive Sciences, 5*(6), 236–243.

Grey, C. (1998). On being a professional in a "Big Six" firm. *Accounting, Organizations and Society, 23*(5–6), 569–587.

Hambrick, D. Z., Macnamara, B. N., Campitelli, G., Ullén, F., & Mosing, M. A. (2016). Beyond born versus made: A new look at expertise. In Ross, B. H. (Ed.). *Psychology of Learning and Motivation* (pp. 1–55). Cambridge, MA: Elsevier Academic Press.

Hodges, N. J., Starkes, J. L., & MacMahon, C. (2006). Expert performance in sport: A cognitive perspective. In Ericsson, K. A., Charness, N., Feltovich,

P. J., & Hoffman, R. R., (Eds.) *The Cambridge Handbook of Expertise and Expert Performance* (pp. 471–488). New York, NY: Cambridge University Press.

Hoffman, R. R. (1998). How can expertise be defined? Implications of research from cognitive psychology. In Williams, R., Faulkner, W., & Fleck, J. (Eds.) *Exploring Expertise* (pp. 81–100). London: Palgrave Macmillan.

Hoffman, R. R. (2019). Identifying experts for the design of human-centered systems, downloaded October 10, 2021, from https://www.ihmc.us/hoffmans-concept-blog/.

Jeon, H. A., Kuhl, U., & Friederici, A. D. (2019). Mathematical expertise modulates the architecture of dorsal and cortico-thalamic white matter tracts. *Scientific Reports, 9*(1), 1–11.

Kahneman, D., & Klein, G. (2009). Conditions for intuitive expertise: A failure to disagree. *American Psychologist, 64*(6), 515–526.

Kay, J., & King, M. (2020). *Radical uncertainty: Decision-making for an unknowable future.* New York, NY: Norton & Company Inc.

Keith, N., & Ericsson, K. A. (2007). A deliberate practice account of typing proficiency in everyday typists. *Journal of Experimental Psychology: Applied, 13*(3), 135–145.

Kellogg, R. T. (2006). Professional writing expertise. In Ericsson, K. A., Charness, N., Feltovich, P.J., & Hoffman, R. R. (Eds.). *The Cambridge Handbook of Expertise and Expert Performance* (pp. 389–402). New York, NY: Cambridge University Press.

Klein, G. A. (2017). *Sources of power: How people make decisions.* Cambridge, MA: MIT Press.

Krampe, R. T., & Charness, N. (2006). Aging and expertise. In Ericsson, K. A., Charness, N., Feltovich, P.J., & Hoffman, R. R., (Eds.). *The Cambridge Handbook of Expertise and Expert Performance* (pp. 723–742). New York, NY: Cambridge University Press.

Lindbeck, A. (2012). *Ekonomi är att välja.* Stockholm: Albert Bonniers Förlag.

Macnamara, B. N., Hambrick, D. Z., & Oswald, F. L. (2014). Deliberate practice and performance in music, games, sports, education, and professions: A meta-analysis. *Psychological Science, 25*(8), 1608–1618.

Macnamara, B. N., Moreau, D., & Hambrick, D. Z. (2016). The relationship between deliberate practice and performance in sports: A meta-analysis. *Perspectives on Psychological Science, 11*(3), 333–350.

Maguire, E. A., Gadian, D. G., Johnsrude, I. S., Good, C. D., Ashburner, J., Frackowiak, R. S., & Frith, C. D. (2000). Navigation-related structural change in the hippocampi of taxi drivers. *Proceedings of the National Academy of Sciences, 97*(8), 4398–4403.

Miller, S. D., Chow, D., Wampold, B. E., Hubble, M. A., Del Re, A. C., Maeschalck, C., & Bargmann, S. (2020). To be or not to be (an expert)? Revisiting the role of deliberate practice in improving performance. *High Ability Studies, 31*(1), 5–15.

Mosing, M. A., Madison, G., Pedersen, N. L., & Ullén, F. (2016). Investigating cognitive transfer within the framework of music practice: Genetic pleiotropy rather than causality. *Developmental Science, 19*(3), 504–512.

OED (2021). Available at: https://www-oed-com/ Accessed October 27, 2021.

Pinho, A. L., de Manzano, Ö., Fransson, P., Eriksson, H., & Ullén, F. (2014). Connecting to create: expertise in musical improvisation is associated with increased functional connectivity between premotor and prefrontal areas. *Journal of Neuroscience, 34*(18), 6156–6163.

Plomin, R., Shakeshaft, N. G., McMillan, A., & Trzaskowski, M. (2014). Nature, nurture, and expertise. *Intelligence, 45,* 46–59.

Polderman, T. J., Benyamin, B., De Leeuw, C. A., Sullivan, P. F., Van Bochoven, A., Visscher, P. M., & Posthuma, D. (2015). Meta-analysis of the heritability of human traits based on fifty years of twin studies. *Nature Genetics, 47*(7), 702–709.

Scholz, J., Klein, M. C., Behrens, T. E., & Johansen-Berg, H. (2009). Training induces changes in white-matter architecture. *Nature Neuroscience, 12*(11), 1370–1371.

Shanteau, J. (1992). Competence in experts: The role of task characteristics. *Organizational Behavior and Human Decision Processes, 53*(2), 252–266.

Shanteau, J. (2015). Why task domains (still) matter for understanding expertise. *Journal of Applied Research in Memory and Cognition, 4*(3), 169–175.

Simon, H. A., & Chase, W. G. (1973). Skill in chess: Experiments with chess-playing tasks and computer simulation of skilled performance throw light on some human perceptual and memory processes. *American Scientist, 61*(4), 394–403.

Taleb, N. N. (2007). *The black swan: The impact of the highly improbable.* New York, NY: Random House.

Tetlock, P. E., & Gardner, D. (2015). *Superforecasting: The art and science of prediction.* New York, NY: Crown.

Thomas, R. P., & Lawrence, A. (2018). Assessment of expert performance compared across professional domains. *Journal of Applied Research in Memory and Cognition, 7*(2), 167–176.

Ullén, F., Hambrick, D. Z., & Mosing, M. A. (2016). Rethinking expertise: A multifactorial gene–environment interaction model of expert performance. *Psychological Bulletin, 142*(4), 427–446.

Voss, J. F., & Wiley, J. (2006). Expertise in history. In Ericsson, K. A., Charness, N., Feltovich, P.J., & Hoffman, R. R. (Eds.). *The Cambridge Handbook of Expertise and Expert Performance* (pp. 569–584). New York, NY: Cambridge University Press.

Ward, P., Gore, J., Hutton, R., Conway, G. E., & Hoffman, R. R. (2018). Adaptive skill as the conditio sine qua non of expertise. *Journal of Applied Research in Memory and Cognition, 7*(1), 35–50.

Ward, P., Schraagen, J. M., Gore, J., & Roth, E. M. (Eds.). (2020). *The Oxford handbook of expertise.* Oxford: Oxford University Press.

Ward, P., & Williams, A. M. (2003). Perceptual and cognitive skill development in soccer: The multidimensional nature of expert performance. *Journal of Sport and Exercise Psychology, 25*(1), 93–111.

Weiss, D. J., & Shanteau, J. (2014). Who's the best? A relativistic view of expertise. *Applied Cognitive Psychology, 28*(4), 447–457.

Winner, E. (2000). The origins and ends of giftedness. *American Psychologist, 55*(1), 159–169.

3 Intuition

This chapter gives an overview of the research on intuition and has three main conclusions. First, intuition can be seen as a judgment arising from nonconscious processes; hence, it is a way of thinking. Dual-process theories describe this as Type 1 processes, that is, intuitive processes that are fast, nonconscious, and automatic. Second, intuition involves emotions. Neurological research shows that emotions are required for rational decision-making, even though too much emotion can lead decision-makers astray. Third, research on Type 1 processes has been dominated by the heuristics and biases program, which stresses that intuitive judgments lead to systematic errors. However, even researchers in that field agree that Type 1 processes supported by expertise typically lead to efficient judgments.

3.1 Defining intuition

Intuition is defined in many different ways (for an overview, see, for example, Akinci & Sadler-Smith, 2012; Dane & Pratt, 2007; Hodgkinson et al., 2008). However, a common view and distinction made by scholars is to separate intuitive processes, or *intuiting*, and the output or product, *intuition* (e.g., Dane &Pratt, 2007; Sinclair, 2020). Listed below, in chronological order, are three definitions commonly used in intuition research.

Hogarth (2001, p. 14) states that intuitions "are reached with little apparent effort, and typically without conscious awareness. They involve little or no conscious deliberation." Later on, Hogarth (2010, p. 339) added that intuitions are typically "correlated with *speed* and often a sense of *confidence* . . . that intuitions are experienced in a *holistic* manner," adding that "intuition is the result of *learning*."

DOI: 10.4324/9781003035725-3

The definition by Hogarth (2001) is broad and covers intuition by both novices and experts, although it can be noted that his book is about improving or "educating" intuition. However, there is a short section on intuition as expertise, linking intuition to a particular domain. He writes (ibid, p. 23): "intuition is like expertise. It is specific to particular domains. It is acquired through domain-relevant experience. And it can be improved through instruction and practice." Hogarth also elaborates on expertise, arguing that the level of expertise or knowledge in domains varies and thus some perform better than others.

Sinclair and Ashkanasy (2005, p. 357) define intuition as "a non-sequential information processing mode, which comprises both cognitive and affective elements and results in direct knowing without any use of conscious reasoning." The definition refers to a holistic processing that is nonlinear and nonsequential in nature. It, like the definition by Hogarth (2001), is rather general and includes intuition by novices as well as experts. Moreover, the definition encompasses "*entrepreneurial intuition* that enables decision makers to connect patterns in a new way" (Sinclair & Ashkanasy, 2005, p. 358).

Dane and Pratt (2007, p. 40) define intuition as "affectively charged judgments that arise through rapid, nonconscious, and holistic associations." Their definition should be viewed in the context of a framework outlining conditions influencing the effective use of intuitive decision-making. These conditions concern the development of expertise in the domain and the character of the task. Consequently, as with the previous two definitions, intuitions by novices as well as experts are within the scope of the definition. However, arguably the holistic associations are likely more related to experts than novices.

In summary, the three definitions are fairly broad. They emphasize that intuitions arise without awareness and in nonconscious processes. Furthermore, intuitions involve an affective element and occur rapidly. Intuition can be distinguished from related concepts such as instincts or insights. Instincts are automatic reflexes, hence they originate from innate capabilities (Hogarth, 2001). Insights are "used to designate the clear and sudden understanding of how to solve a problem" (Bowden et al., 2005, p. 322), which involves an incubation period. Even though the authors describe the importance of experience or expertise, their definitions are general enough to include intuitions based on limited or no experience, corresponding to the left-hand circle in Figure 1.1.

In this book, we will use the definition by Dane and Pratt (2007) to describe intuitions. Of the three definitions presented, it is the latest and most developed one. It is also accompanied by an elaborate framework, which includes propositions, and it is based on research in intuition and expertise. Hence, we find it suitable to discuss and analyze the use of intuition in broader domains of expertise, such as those of CFOs, CEOs, and other senior executives. In the following two sections, we will discuss two fundamental characteristics of intuiting and intuitions, that is, affective elements and nonconscious processes.

3.2 Emotions and affect

The role of emotions or affect[1] in judgments and decisions is sometimes portrayed in contrast to reason and rationality. Reason and rationality represent optimal decisions, as opposed to affect-laden "poor" decisions. However, current knowledge suggests that the emotional system is a prerequisite for effective judgments and decisions, especially those comprising risk and ambiguities. Consequently, and as discussed in the previous section, the definition of intuition by Dane and Pratt (2007), like the one by Sinclair and Ashkanasy (2005), includes affective elements. Dane and Pratt (2007. p. 38) write: "We further clarify intuitive judgments as 'affectively charged' given that such judgments often involve emotions." Still, to provide a deeper understanding of the role of emotions in intuitions, in the following, we will draw on research in neuroscience and on the somatic[2] marker hypothesis (Damasio, 1994; Damasio et al., 1991).

The neural systems of emotion and feeling have developed sequentially over time, responding to what is "good for life" and "bad for life." Damasio (2003, p. 80) explains:

The first device, emotion, enabled organisms to respond effectively but not creatively to a number of circumstances conducive or threatening to life—'good for life' or 'bad for life' circumstances, 'good for life' or 'bad for life' outcomes. The second device feeling, introduced a mental alert for the good or bad circumstances and prolonged the impact of emotions by affecting attention and memory lastingly. This happens in both animals and humans. Eventually in a fruitful combination with past memories, imagination, and reasoning, feelings led to the emergence of foresight and the possibility to create novel, non-stereotypical responses.

Emotions represent specific neural systems developed over time, whereas feelings are perceptions of the emotional state. The emotional system can be triggered by innate or learned stimuli, or something that is recalled from memory or a hypothetical event (Bechara & Damasio, 2005). Jumping when seeing a snake is obviously an innate trigger, while joy when passing an exam is learned. Memories from a pleasant holiday are an example of a trigger from memory. An example of a trigger from a hypothetical event is fretting about a loss of money.

That emotions are related to neural systems, and their functioning has been extensively tested in experiments. One prominent example is Bechara et al. (1997), who studied patients with damage to regions of the brain associated with emotions. The findings were reported in their article: "Deciding advantageously before knowing the advantageous strategy." It provides a basis for the earlier developed somatic marker hypothesis and provides an illustration of it. The illustration consists of a famous experiment, the so-called "Iowa gambling task."

In this experiment, patients, with lesions to the parts of the brain associated with emotions, are compared with a control group of ordinary people. The comparison was possible by observing how the participants responded to a game. It needs to be pointed out that the patients in all other ways functioned normally, had high IQ scores, and could solve logical problems. The players were presented four decks of cards with the goal to earn as much as possible. The first two decks (A and B) yielded high gains ($100) and losses (−$100), and they ultimately led to a loss; however, the other two decks (C and D) yielded lower gains ($50) and losses (−$50), and they ultimately led to a gain. The participants were provided a loan of $2,000. In total, 100 cards were drawn by each participant. After a certain number of cards were drawn, the participants were asked two questions: "i) Tell me all you know about what is going on in this game, ii) Tell me how you feel about this game" (p. 1293). To measure bodily related responses (somatic), Skin Conductance Responses (SCRs) were used as a marker.[3]

After picking a few cards with losses, the control group started to show SCRs and avoided decks with large losses. Yet they could still not tell what was going on. After about 50 cards, they got a "hunch" that decks A and B were riskier. By card 80, many of them expressed knowledge about why decks C and D were better than decks A and B. In stark contrast to this outcome, none of the patients participating in the experiment generated a bodily response through SCR. Furthermore, patients who could accurately describe the bad and the good decks still continued to choose the bad decks. Hence, they failed to choose the right decks even though they had the knowledge.

The somatic marker hypothesis (Bechara & Damasio, 2005; Damasio, 1994; Damasio et al., 1991) provides an explanation to the findings described above. Bechara and Damasio (2005, p. 336) write:

> *The key idea of this hypothesis is that decision-making is a process that is influenced by marker signals that arise in bioregulatory processes, including those that express themselves in emotions and feelings. This influence can occur at multiple levels of operation, some of which occur consciously, and some of which occur non-consciously.*

Hence, the neural system of emotion reacts to right and wrong decisions, picking the right deck of cards after a period of implicit learning. The reaction is seen by marker signals, operationalized through SCRs. This guides the decision to pick a card from the right deck, even though the person does not need to be consciously aware of it.

Taken together, the neurological research adds several insights to the role of emotion and intuition, especially in complex situations with risk and ambiguities. This can be illustrated in three different ways. First, as Bechara and Damasio (2005, p. 352) describe it:

> *The somatic marker hypothesis provides neurobiological evidence in support of the notion that people often make judgments based on 'hunches', 'gut feelings' and subjective evaluation of consequences.*

In other words, subjective evaluations (i.e., emotions) guide decisions. For example, in the card game above, the participants' emotional system reacted and guided the right move and decision, even prior to participants becoming consciously aware of how the game worked. The participants unconsciously learned the right move after drawing a certain number of cards.

In a similar manner, an expert, after years of experience, has learned, explicitly and implicitly, what is good and bad performance. This process of learning is guided by previous experience and manifested in the use of intuitive judgments. On a more speculative note, this might also explain why a long period of experience is required to acquire expertise. If a person has not been exposed to a specific situation— figuratively "not drawn a card from any of the decks"—their system of emotion has probably not had the time to develop a suitable response (see also Zweig, 2002, for investment decisions in stocks).

Second, emotions can be unconscious. Thus, intuitions do not need to be accompanied by a feeling of emotion. The statement by Dane and Pratt (2007) of intuitions as "affectively charged" does not need to be something that people are aware of. This can also be observed in studies of intuitive expertise where affect has not necessarily been consciously felt (e.g., Grant & Nilsson, 2020; Huang, 2018; Huang & Pearce, 2015).

Third, emotions may not always be beneficial to decision-making. Two examples of this are going into a meeting in an angry state, or recalling a previous negative emotional event, unrelated to the decision at hand. In both these examples, emotions can have a negative effect on both judgments and decisions. Studies also support that triggered positive emotional states can strengthen biases, such as overconfidence (Ifcher & Zarghamee, 2014). Evidently, awareness of how emotional states not related to the task at hand can affect judgments and decisions is critical. This also provides support to the old saying "sleep on it" before making an important decision.

3.3 Dual-process theories

Most research in the field of intuition builds on dual-process theories of thinking to explain the underlying cognitive processes of intuition (Ashkanasy & Sinclair, 2005; Dane & Pratt, 2007; Hodgkinson & Sadler-Smith, 2018; Kahneman, 2011; Kahneman & Klein, 2009).[4] Dual-process theories concern, for example, reasoning, judgment, and decision-making, and they can be described as "a class of theories in which two fundamentally different types of cognitive processes are distinguished" (Pennycook et al., 2018, p. 667). One type can be described as being intuitive, fast, automatic, and unconscious and the other as being analytical, slow, deliberate, and conscious (Evans, 2008; Kahneman, 2011).

The idea of dual aspects of the mind has a long background spanning back from Aristotle (Sloman, 1996), Freud (Epstein, 1994) and to the last decades of research in cognitive and social psychology (Evans, 2008; Evans & Stanovich, 2013a; Hodgkinson & Sadler-Smith, 2018). Today, dual-process theories have strong support from research in the psychological field and are in line with recent research in neuroscience (Lieberman, 2007). However, as noted above, the dual-process concept is not unequivocal but rather includes a class of theories, which have been described with different terms and characteristics. A common description is the concept of System 1 and System 2 (Epstein, 1994: Stanovich, 1999; Kahneman, 2011). In this book, we follow the terminology recently suggested by Evans and Stanovich (2013a) and call the processes Type 1 and Type 2 to avoid mistaking them for the two-minds hypotheses, that is, the notion that there are only two systems underlying these processes. For example, Type 1 can be seen as a set of systems rather than one (Stanovich, 2011).

Following different dual-process theories, Type 1 and Type 2 processes have been named and characterized in several different ways (for overviews, see, for example, Evans, 2008; Evans & Stanovich, 2013a; Hodgkinson & Sadler-Smith, 2018). In a recent review, Evans and Stanovich (2013a) cluster characteristics of Type 1 and Type 2 processes in two groups, one defining features and the other identifying typical correlates. The authors argue that the distinguishing feature of a Type 1 process (intuitive) is that it "[d]oes not require working memory, [and is] autonomous" (p. 225). They further state that Type 1 processes "do not require 'controlled attention' which is another way of saying that they make minimal demands on working memory" (p. 236). Examples of correlates for Type 1 processes are: fast, nonconscious, automatic, and associative.

The defining features of Type 2 processes (reflective) are similar but in an opposing manner. They relate to working memory and "controlled attention," as suggested by Evans and Stanovich. Hence, the definition of Type 2 processes is: "Requires working memory [and] Cognitive decoupling; mental simulation" (p. 225). The cognitive decoupling means the abstract thinking that is necessary for hypothetical thought. Moreover, Type 2 processing "enables uniquely human facilities, such as hypothetical thinking, mental simulation and consequential decision making"[5] (Evans & Stanovich, 2013a, p. 235). Examples of correlates for Type 2 processes are: slow, conscious, controlled, and rule based.

To explain the interaction between Type 1 and Type 2 processes, dual-process theories focus on different cognitive mechanisms. Two of the most commonly used mechanisms are found in the partly opposing default-interventionist model (Evans, 2007, 2008; Evans & Stanovich, 2013a; Kahneman and Frederick, 2002; Stanovich & West, 2000) and the parallel model (Epstein, 1994; Hodgkinson & Sadler-Smith, 2018; Lieberman, 2000, 2007; Sloman, 1996). Several dual-process theories have adhered to the former of these two models. Lately, researchers have made a case for the latter model, arguing that it supports research findings in management and organization studies (Hodgkinson & Sadler-Smith, 2018). Evans (2007, p. 321) describes the two models as follows:

> The parallel-competitive model *assumes that each system operates in parallel to deliver a putative response, resulting sometimes in conflict that then needs to be resolved. . . . the default-interventionist model involves the cueing of default responses by the heuristic system that may or may not be altered by subsequent intervention of the analytic system.*
> (underlined words are italicized in the original text)

The default-interventionist model, which many researchers use (e.g., Evans, 2008; Evans & Stanovich, 2013a; Kahneman & Frederick, 2002; Stanovich & West, 2000), is based on the idea that the default response (e.g., answer, judgment, or decision) is produced by Type 1 processes. Type 2 processes might or might not override the initial Type 1 response. This is also, as Evans and Stanovich note (2013a), in line with Kahneman (2011), and the view that humans are cognitive misers. Thus, they tend to use Type 1 processes when making judgments and decisions. A reason is that most of the time we cannot afford to use the slow and effortful processes of Type 2.

The parallel-competitive model assumes that Type 1 and Type 2 processes work in parallel and can interact and cooperate. When they are in conflict, "resolution occurs after heuristics [Type 1 processes] and analytic [Type 2] processes each have proposed a response" (Evans, 2007, p. 327). Hence, Type 1 and Type 2 processes compete for the answer; however, when there are conflicts, for example, the feeling says something, and the analysis says something else, both intuitive and analytical responses are considered.

The different and opposing arguments regarding the parallel and the default-interventionist model make some researchers unsure as to which is the right one to use. For example, Evans (2007, p. 336) describes his doubts about whether the default-interventionist model is always the right approach:

> *Although I prefer the default-interventionist approach in my own revised heuristic-analytic theory of reasoning (Evans, 2006b), this may not be the correct approach for all the various dual-processing accounts in psychology to take.*

In line with this, Hodgkinson and Sadler-Smith (2018, p. 485), who are proponents of the parallel model, speculate that both models could prove to be helpful in our understanding of the interaction between Type 1 and Type 2 processes:

> *... perhaps each variant might prove more or less influential in particular topic areas over the longer term.*

The default-interventionist model is favored among dual-process researchers, as well as heuristics and biases researchers. This model typically uses heuristics and is, thus, open for systematic errors or biases. However, the parallel model seems more relevant to use in a managerial and organizational context (see, for example, Hodgkinson and Sadler-Smith, 2018) and especially when analyzing decisions by professionals with expertise. Nonetheless, and as described in the following section, experts such as auditors and CFOs are not immune to heuristics and biases, including overconfidence.

3.4 Heuristics and biases

Research on Type 1 processes and intuitions has been, and partly still is, dominated by the heuristics and biases research program, which was established in the early 1970s by Amos Tversky and Daniel Kahneman and their article "Judgment under uncertainty: Heuristics and biases" (Tversky & Kahneman, 1974).[6] This research focuses on when the use of Type 1 processes can lead to systematic errors, so-called "biases." The following section is a brief description of the development in heuristics and biases research. Our account is primarily based on the works by Kahneman and his colleagues.

The heuristics and biases research program both influenced and was influenced by the development of dual-process theories. For example, a key question for researchers studying dual processes is to comprehend interrelations and dynamics when there is conflict between Type 1 and Type 2 processes. This typically emanates from the quest to understand and explain classic tasks from heuristics and biases research such as representativeness and the conjunction fallacy, for example, "the Linda problem" or "the bat and the ball problem" (De Neys, 2014).[7] Furthermore, heuristics and biases researchers incorporated findings on dual-process theories into their work (Kahneman & Frederick, 2002).

In their 1974 article, Tversky and Kahneman state that people use heuristics, that is, mental shortcuts that simplify complex tasks into simpler operations. They categorize findings by three heuristic principles: representativeness, availability, and adjustment and anchoring. Together, they encompass a dozen systematic errors or biases. Representativeness is heuristics focusing on similarity rather than probabilities. Tversky and Kahneman (1974, pp. 1127–1128) describe availability, and adjustment and anchoring in the following way:

> ... the ease with which instances or occurrences can be brought to mind. For example, one may assess the risk of heart attack among middle-aged people by recalling such occurrences among one's acquaintances.
>
> ... people make estimates starting from an initial value that is adjusted to yield the final answer ... That is, different starting points yield different estimates, which are biased toward the initial value. We call this phenomenon anchoring.

At the time of the 1974 article, dual-process theories had not yet developed. As the heuristics and biases research program proceeded, dual-process theories progressed. In 2000, Kahneman read and was heavily influenced by an article by Stanovich and West (2000) outlining what they named System 1 and System 2 processes of thinking (Kahneman, 2011). Subsequently, Kahneman and Frederick (2002) incorporated dual-process theories in their research program, adhering to a default-interventionist model. The underlying view was that people tend to seek out quick solutions, that is, use Type 1 processes to make judgments or seek solutions to problems. Making biases disappear is a task for Type 2 processes, requiring these to intervene and override the initial intuitive response. According to Kahneman and Frederick (2002, p. 69), this depends on:

> *. . . cognitive skills (education, intelligence) and on formulations that make the applicability of a rule apparent (frequency format) or a relevant factor more salient (manipulations of attention). We assume that intuitions are less sensitive to these factors, and that the appearance or disappearance of biases mainly reflects variations in the efficacy of corrective operations.*

The findings on the reduction or elimination of biases described in the quote above refer to the studies on factors affecting the outcome of typical heuristic experiments and problems, for example, the above-mentioned "Linda problem" and "the bat and the ball problem." One factor that reduces or eliminates systematic errors is cognitive skills, and education or expertise in an area. For example, statistical skills reduce errors in statistical problems, such as the "Linda problem" (Nisbett et al., 1983). How problems are formulated also affects the outcome, for example, probabilities such as 0.05 are harder to understand than 1 in 20. Furthermore, manipulating attention, for example by asking participants in experiments to think as a statistician rather than a psychologist, reduces systematic errors (Zukier & Pepitone, 1984).

A further development by Kahneman and Frederick (2002) concerned the heuristics construct, which became much more clearly defined based on attribute substitution. The definition encompassed representativeness and availability heuristics; however, anchoring did not qualify as a heuristic. Furthermore, Kahneman and Frederick added an affect heuristic in line with the increasing attention to emotions in psychology. The new definition of the heuristic construct was described in the following way (Kahneman & Frederick, 2002, p. 53):

> *We will say that judgment is mediated by a heuristic when an individual assesses a specified* target attribute *of a judgment object by substituting another property of that object—*the heuristic attribute*—which comes more readily to mind. Many judgments are made by this process of* attribute substitution.
>
> (underlined words are italicized in the original text)

In summary, the heuristics and biases program has identified and increased the understanding of how our thinking can lead to systematic errors, biases (for an overview, see, for example, Bazerman & Moore, 2012; Kahneman, 2011; Stanovich et al., 2016). However, researchers involved in this program still seem to agree that most of our intuitions and heuristics are typically useful and do not lead to systematic errors. This is also disclosed in the seminal works by Kahneman and colleagues discussed above, and in later works, as illustrated by the following quotes:

> *This article shows that people rely on a limited number of heuristic principles which reduce the complex tasks of assessing probabilities and predicting values to simpler judgmental operations. In general, these heuristics are quite useful, but sometimes they lead to severe and systematic errors.*
>
> (Tversky & Kahneman, 1974, p. 1124)

> *The study of biases is compatible with a view of intuitive thinking and decision making as generally skilled and successful.*
>
> (Kahneman, 2003, p. 697)

> *We did not ask ourselves whether all intuitive judgments under uncertainty are produced by the heuristics we studied; it is now clear that they are not. In particular, the accurate intuitions of experts are better explained by the effects of prolonged practice than by heuristics. We can now draw a richer and more balanced picture, in which skill and heuristics are alternative sources of intuitive judgments and choices.*
>
> (Kahneman, 2011, p. 11)

The last quote is from the book *Thinking Fast and Slow* by Daniel Kahneman (2011). It can be seen as a summary of his heuristics and biases research since it started more than 5 decades ago. Daniel Kahneman is one of the most prominent researchers in the field and became a Nobel laureate in 2002. In the quote, he reflects on judgments and decisions based on intuitions and where heuristics and systematic errors can be placed in the wider context of intuitive processes in general, and intuitions by people with certain skills in particular. This suggests, as we will discuss in the next chapter, that expert intuitions typically lead to efficient judgments and decision, in contrast to heuristics leading to biases. However, experts such as top managers are, obviously, not immune to mistakes. Overconfidence is a salient example that Kahneman and others have observed in this category of people, leading to poor judgments and decisions (e.g., Kahneman, 2011; Malmendier & Tate, 2005; Roll, 1986).

3.5 Summary

Intuitions are the output or product of internal processes of intuiting. Two fundamental characteristics of intuitions and intuiting are the affective elements and the nonconscious processes. Hence, to understand the role of intuition in judgments and decisions, we need to have a framework of the role of emotions and how we think.

Studies in neuroscience show that emotions guide decisions, especially those involving risk and ambiguities. Furthermore, these studies show that emotions can be at an unconscious level. For example, in the card task presented above, the participants' emotional system reacted and guided the right move and decision, prior to the participants becoming consciously aware of them (Bechara et al., 1997). The participants implicitly learned the right move after drawing a certain number of cards. In a similar manner, a university professor or CFO, after being exposed to years of experience, has implicitly and explicitly learned what is good and bad in their respective tasks. Hence, they are using intuitive judgments guided by their previous experience.

Dual-process theories provide an explanation to how we think, for example, reasoning, judgment, and decision-making. Type 1 processes provide an explanation of the internal process of intuiting that precedes the intuition. These processes do not require working memory and can be described as being intuitive, fast, nonconscious, automatic, and associative. Type 2 processes require working memory and abstract thinking necessary for hypothetical thoughts and can be described as being slow, conscious, controlled, and rule based.

There are different explanations of how Type 1 and Type 2 processes interact. Two salient models are the default-interventionist and the parallel-competitive models. We adhere to a parallel-competitive model, where intuitive and analytical processes are used interactively in a complementary way, and, in times of conflict, compete. The reason is that this model seems to offer a more realistic view of understanding, judgments, and decisions in the managerial and organizational context.

Research on Type 1 processes has been, and partly still is, dominated by the heuristics and biases research program, examining when intuitive judgments or decisions lead to flawed outcomes. However, even Daniel Kahneman, the most influential researcher in this program, recognizes that expert intuitions, typically in contrast to heuristics, lead to efficient judgments and decisions. However, experts and top managers are, obviously, not immune to mistakes, regardless of whether you are a university professor or a CFO. A salient example, especially among top managers, is overconfidence leading to poor judgments and decisions.

Notes

1 Dane and Pratt (2007) and Sinclair and Ashkanasy (2005) use affect and emotions interchangeably. In intuition research, affect seems to be a frequently used term (e.g., Akinci & Sadler-Smith, 2011). However, in psychology, affect is a broader term that encompasses feelings and emotions (APA, 2021). In this section, we will distinguish between the terms emotion and feeling.

2 The term somatic means describing, relating to, or arising in the body rather than from the mind (APA, 2021). The term originates from the Greek word soma, which means body.

3 A typical emotional response is skin conductance. It consists of sweating controlled by the sympathetic nervous system, which is seen as a measure of emotional and sympathetic responses.

4 Two other major explanations of decision-making and cognition are researched by Gigerenzer and colleagues, focusing on fast and frugal heuristics (Gigerenzer & Todd, 1999), and Klein and colleagues, focusing on recognition-primed decision-making (Klein, 2017). See Evans and Stanovich (2013b) and Hodgkinson & Sadler-Smith (2018) for a discussion.

5 Consequential decision-making can be described as "choices that are determined by reasoning about or simulation of future consequences of anticipated actions, as opposed to choices driven by experiential learning and associative strength" (Evans, 2008, p. 238).

6 The program started in 1969 with a questionnaire-based survey of professional psychologists. The participants were asked statistical questions concerning research decisions. The findings showed that even psychologists with statistical expertise showed erroneous statistical intuitions (Tversky & Kahneman, 1971).

7 "The Linda problem" and "the bat and the ball problem" are classical examples from heuristics and biases research showing how the use of intuition can lead to erroneous answers.

The Linda problem was set up as follows. First respondents were provided information about Linda, thereafter they were asked questions about her. Linda is described as: "31 years old, single, outspoken and very bright. She majored in philosophy. As a student she was deeply concerned with issues of discrimination and social justice and also participated in antinuclear demonstrations." (Kahneman, 2003, p. 1462). Respondents were asked what employment Linda has. Eight alternatives were provided, of which the two critical were whether she was a bank teller only or whether she was both a bank teller and active in the feminist movement. The respondents mostly choose the option that she was both a bank teller and active in the feminist movement. This indicates an intuitive response. The answer that she is representative of, or similar to, a bank teller and active in the feminist movement seems reasonable for a judgment using similarities, whereas a judgment based on probabilities would rank the answer of only being a bank teller higher.

The bat and the ball problem is described by Kahneman and Frederick (2002, p. 58): "A bat and a ball cost $1.10 in total. The bat costs $1 more than the ball. How much does the ball cost? Almost everyone we ask reports an initial tendency to answer 10 cents because the sum $1.10 separates naturally into $1 and 10 cents, and 10 cents is about the right magnitude. Many people yield to this immediate impulse".

References

Akinci, C., & Sadler-Smith, E. (2012). Intuition in management research: A historical review. *International Journal of Management Reviews*, *14*(1), 104–122.

APA (2021). Available at: https://dictionary.apa.org/ Accessed October 27, 2021.

Bazerman, M. H., & Moore, D. A. (2012). *Judgment in managerial decision making*. New York, NY: John Wiley & Sons.

Bechara, A., & Damasio, A. R. (2005). The somatic marker hypothesis: A neural theory of economic decision. *Games and Economic Behavior*, *52*(2), 336–372.

Bechara, A., Damasio, H., Tranel, D., & Damasio, A. R. (1997). Deciding advantageously before knowing the advantageous strategy. *Science*, *275*(5304), 1293–1295.

Bowden, E. M., Jung-Beeman, M., Fleck, J., & Kounios, J. (2005). New approaches to demystifying insight. *Trends in Cognitive Sciences*, *9*(7), 322–328.

Damasio, A. R. (1994). *Descartes' error: Emotion, reason, and the human brain*. New York, NY: Grosset/Putnam.

Damasio, A. R. (2003). *Looking for Spinoza: Joy, sorrow, and the feeling brain*. New York, NY: Houghton Mifflin Harcourt.

Damasio, A. R., Tranel, D., & Damasio, H. C. (1991). Somatic markers and the guidance of behaviour: Theory and preliminary testing. In Levin, H. M., Eisenberg, H. M., & Benton, A. L. (Eds.), *Frontal Lobe Function and Dysfunction*, (pp. 217–229). Oxford: Oxford University Press.

Dane, E., & Pratt, M. G. (2007). Exploring intuition and its role in managerial decision making. *Academy of Management Review*, *32*(1), 33–54.

De Neys, W. (2014). Conflict detection, dual processes, and logical intuitions: Some clarifications. *Thinking & Reasoning, 20*(2), 169–187.

Epstein, S. (1994). Integration of the cognitive and the psychodynamic unconscious. *American Psychologist, 49*(8), 709–724.

Evans, J. S. B. (2006b). The heuristic-analytic theory of reasoning: Extension and evaluation. *Psychonomic Bulletin and Review, 13*(3), 378–395.

Evans, J. S. B. (2007). On the resolution of conflict in dual process theories of reasoning. *Thinking & Reasoning, 13*(4), 321–339.

Evans, J. S. B. (2008). Dual-processing accounts of reasoning, judgment, and social cognition. *Annual Review of Psychology, 59*, 255–278.

Evans, J. S. B., & Stanovich, K. E. (2013a). Dual-process theories of higher cognition: Advancing the debate. *Perspectives on Psychological Science, 8*(3), 223–241.

Evans, J. S. B., & Stanovich, K. E. (2013b). Theory and metatheory in the study of dual processing: Reply to comments. *Perspectives on Psychological Science, 8*(3), 263–271.

Gigerenzer, G., & Todd, P. M. (1999). *Simple heuristics that make us smart.* New York, NY: Oxford University Press.

Grant, M., & Nilsson, F. (2020). The production of strategic and financial rationales in capital investments: Judgments based on intuitive expertise. *The British Accounting Review, 52*(3), 100861.

Hodgkinson, G. P., Langan-Fox, J., & Sadler-Smith, E. (2008). Intuition: A fundamental bridging construct in the behavioural sciences. *British Journal of Psychology, 99*(1), 1–27.

Hodgkinson, G. P., & Sadler-Smith, E. (2018). The dynamics of intuition and analysis in managerial and organizational decision making. *Academy of Management Perspectives, 32*(4), 473–492.

Hogarth, R. M. (2001). *Educating intuition.* Chicago, IL: University of Chicago Press.

Hogarth, R. M. (2010). Intuition: A challenge for psychological research on decision making. *Psychological Inquiry, 21*(4), 338–353.

Huang, L. (2018). The role of investor gut feel in managing complexity and extreme risk. *Academy of Management Journal, 61*(5), 1821–1847.

Huang, L., & Pearce, J. L. (2015). Managing the unknowable: The effectiveness of early-stage investor gut feel in entrepreneurial investment decisions. *Administrative Science Quarterly, 60*(4), 634–670.

Ifcher, J., & Zarghamee, H. (2014). Affect and overconfidence: A laboratory investigation. *Journal of Neuroscience, Psychology, and Economics, 7*(3), 125–150.

Kahneman, D. (2003). A perspective on judgment and choice: Mapping bounded rationality. *American Psychologist, 58*(9), 697–720.

Kahneman, D. (2011). *Thinking, fast and slow.* New York, NY: Farrar, Straus and Giroux.

Kahneman, D., & Frederick, S. (2002). Representativeness revisited: Attribute substitution in intuitive judgment. In Gilovich, T., Griffin, D. & Kahneman, D. (Eds), *Heuristics and Biases: The Psychology of Intuitive Judgment* (pp. 49–81). New York, NY: Cambridge University Press.

Kahneman, D., & Klein, G. (2009). Conditions for intuitive expertise: A failure to disagree. *American Psychologist, 64*(6), 515–526.

Klein, G. A. (2017). *Sources of power: How people make decisions.* Cambridge, MA: MIT Press.

Lieberman, M. D. (2000). Intuition: a social cognitive neuroscience approach. *Psychological Bulletin, 126*(1), 109.

Lieberman, M. D. (2007). Social cognitive neuroscience: A review of core processes. *Annual Review of Psychology, 58,* 259–289.

Malmendier, U., & Tate, G. (2005). CEO overconfidence and corporate investment. *The Journal of Finance, 60*(6), 2661–2700.

Nisbett, R. E., Krantz, D. H., Jepson, C., & Kunda, Z. (1983). The use of statistical heuristics in everyday inductive reasoning. *Psychological Review, 90*(4), 339–363.

Pennycook, G., De Neys, W., Evans, J. S. B., Stanovich, K. E., & Thompson, V. A. (2018). The mythical dual-process typology. *Trends in Cognitive Sciences, 22*(8), 667–668.

Roll, R. (1986). The hubris hypothesis of corporate takeovers. *The Journal of Business,* 59(2), 197–216.

Sinclair, M. (2020). An introduction to intuition theory and practice: A summary and a research agenda. In Sinclair, M. (Ed.). *Handbook of Intuition Research as Practice* (pp. xix–xxii). Cheltenham: Edward Elgar Publishing.

Sinclair, M., & Ashkanasy, N. M. (2005). Intuition: Myth or a decision-making tool? *Management Learning, 36*(3), 353–370.

Sloman, S. A. (1996). The empirical case for two systems of reasoning. *Psychological Bulletin, 119*(1), 3–22.

Stanovich, K. E. (1999). *Who is rational?: Studies of individual differences in reasoning.* Mahwah, NJ: Psychology Press.

Stanovich, K. E. (2011). *Rationality and the reflective mind.* New York, NY: Oxford University Press.

Stanovich, K. E., & West, R. F. (2000). Individual differences in reasoning: Implications for the rationality debate? *Behavioral and Brain Sciences, 23*(5), 645–665.

Stanovich, K. E., West, R. F., & Toplak, M. E. (2016). *The rationality quotient: Toward a test of rational thinking.* Cambridge, MA: MIT Press.

Tversky, A., & Kahneman, D. (1971). Belief in the law of small numbers. *Psychological bulletin, 76*(2), 105–110.

Tversky, A., & Kahneman, D. (1974). Judgment under uncertainty: Heuristics and biases. *Science, 185*(4157), 1124–1131.

Zukier, H., & Pepitone, A. (1984). Social roles and strategies in prediction: Some determinants of the use of base-rate information. *Journal of Personality and Social Psychology, 47*(2), 349–360.

Zweig, J. (2002). Are you wired for wealth? *Money, 31*(10), 74–81.

4   Intuitive expertise

This chapter provides an overview of theories of intuitive expertise as well as empirical field studies. The chapter has three main conclusions. First, intuitive expertise relates to how experts draw on expertise when using intuition. Hence, it combines intuition with expertise. Second, intuitive expertise is effective for judgmental tasks, that is, tasks characterized by a high level of uncertainty, not solved by unambiguous analytical solutions. Third, field studies support that intuitive expertise is effective in financial decision-making. Simultaneously, they show how intuitive expertise can be successfully combined with analysis. Hence, intuitive and analytical processes should be seen as complementary in financial decision-making, in contrast to the frequently portrayed dichotomy of using either intuitive or analytical processes.

4.1   Defining intuitive expertise

Intuitive expertise is a combination of intuition and expertise, as illustrated in Figure 1.1. It can be seen as the capacity to intuitively "draw on our domain specific knowledge in the form of expertise accumulated in the past" (Sinclair, 2010, p. 382). Hence, it has to do with an expert's use of intuition.

One of the few articles where intuitive expertise is specifically deliberated is by Kahneman and Klein (2009).[1] Their paper is the result of several years of discussions between the two researchers. Kahneman, as described in Chapter 3, represents the heuristics and biases research and is one of its founders. His research on intuitive expertise is primarily related to when judgments based on intuitions can lead to systematic errors (biases). Klein, on the other hand, is one of

DOI: 10.4324/9781003035725-4

the founders of the naturalistic decision-making tradition. This field of research focuses on experiences and skills in naturalistic settings, as opposed to the experimental design common in heuristics and biases research. Thus, naturalistic decision-making examines judgments and decisions leading to efficient outcomes.

Even though these researchers represent two different traditions and perspectives, they found, to their own surprise, an agreement on the conditions of intuitive expertise. The conditions that they outline for intuitive judgments to be skilled build on theories of dual processes, validity of the environment, and the ability to acquire expertise. In essence, they build this on knowledge from the two separate areas of intuition and expertise. In the following, we will discuss these conditions in relation to our previous chapters, modifying and adding to the conditions identified by Kahneman and Klein (2009).

Kahneman and Klein do not expand on the dual-process theories. However, in other writings (Kahneman, 2011; Kahneman & Frederick, 2002), Kahneman has explained that his view is based on the default-interventionist model, which means that the intuitive process is the default that might be overrun by analytical thinking. In contrast to this, and as discussed in the Chapter 3, we adhere to the parallel competitive model (i.e., that there is interaction between analytical and intuitive thinking). An explanation for this choice is that the setting we study is managerial decision-making. These decisions take place over a long period of time and consist of a multitude of judgments and decisions, characteristics that are difficult to replicate in an experimental setting (Hodgkinson & Sadler-Smith, 2018).

Kahneman and Klein (2009, p. 520) describe validity of the environment and the individual's ability to acquire expertise as follows:

> *First, the environment must provide adequately valid cues to the nature of the situation. Second, people must have an opportunity to learn the relevant cues.*

Hence, sufficient environmental regularities are a requisite. Kahneman and Klein define validity as "the causal and statistical structure of the relevant environment" (ibid.). However, they recognize that high validity does not preclude uncertainties. This resonates well with the more detailed discussion in Chapter 2, where we describe how expertise is dependent on domain and task characteristics, and that domains can be more or less benign to expertise. Furthermore, adding to Kahneman and Klein (2009), we suggest that domains and tasks are dynamic and develop. For example, through advances in our knowledge and the tools used, domains and tasks mature and can become more benign for expertise.

Moreover, Kahneman and Klein (2009) point out that people must have an opportunity to learn, referring to motivation and the deliberate practice literature (Ericsson, 2006; Ericsson et al., 2006). However, they do not develop this further. In our chapter on expertise, we add to their paper by outlining the present knowledge of how expertise can be developed and what personal characteristics are favorable. This involves neural and memory mechanisms that are necessary in the process of acquiring expertise. A further conclusion from the chapter is that a long period of deliberate practice is required to become an expert, typically 10 years or more. Repeating tasks and getting feedback is necessary, as well as being exposed to challenging tasks. To meet these demanding requirements, motivation and strong perseverance are needed. These traits are also required for upholding expertise over a long period of time.

4.2 Conditions for effective use of intuitive expertise

A key question is: Under what conditions is intuitive expertise more efficient than analytical processes? We have previously described how the characteristics of domain and task affect whether they are benign for expertise. Dane and Pratt (2007) argue that the character of the task affects how effective intuition is. This adds to the understanding of intuitive expertise and to the framework developed by Kahneman and Klein (2009). Thus, even if an area is benign for expertise, the character of the task determines whether the use of intuitive expertise is effective. For example, engineering problems, such as assessing the capacity of a highway, are better solved with analytical reasoning than intuitive judgment (Hammond et al., 1987). On the other hand, behavioral judgments, such as judging confession statements, are better solved with intuitive processes (Albrechtsen et al., 2009). In the following, we will discuss this in detail, drawing on experimental studies that examine the relationship between task characteristics and the use of intuitive and analytical judgments.

Several studies of judgmental tasks,[2] typically using students (i.e., nonexperts as participants), show that intuitive judgments lead to better outcomes than analytical judgments. These studies are often conducted by splitting participants into two groups. In essence, one group is instructed to base their judgment on careful analysis, whereas the other group is instructed or induced to base their judgment on intuition. Examples of judgmental tasks used in these studies are judgment of confession statements (Albrechtsen et al., 2009) and judgments of the quality of items such as food, paintings, advertisements, and apartments (McMackin & Slovic, 2000; Nordgren & Dijksterhuis, 2009; Nordgren et al., 2011; Wilson & Schooler, 1991). Wilson and Schooler (1991) suggest that an explanation for the inferior performance of analytical processes might be that people focus on salient and plausible factors that can be described or articulated. In a similar way, Nordgren and Dijksterhuis (2009) argue that deliberation distracts attention in another direction than the most relevant ones (see also Lane & Schooler, 2004).

There are a few studies examining experts' use of intuitive judgments and task characteristics (Dane et al., 2012; Dijkstra et al., 2013; Hammond et al., 1987). These studies show that for judgmental tasks the use of intuitive expertise outperforms analytical judgments or solutions. Examples of tasks used in these studies are judgments of aesthetics of highways, difficulty of basketball shots, authenticity of brand handbags, and quality of paintings. As noted by Dane et al. (2012), these tasks cannot be considered as demanding as, for example, financial decision-making. The reason is that tasks such as financial decisions-making have a multitude of alternatives and outcomes, which makes it very difficult to determine the best cause for action.

Hammond et al. (1987) only studied experts, that is, expert highway engineers, and did not investigate the differences between them and novices. The other two studies mentioned above used undergraduate students and classified those with some experience of the task as experts. In contrast to the findings described from the studies, with nonexpert participants (i.e., Albrechtsen et al., 2009; McMackin & Slovic, 2000; Nordgren & Dijksterhuis, 2009; Nordgren et al., 2011; Wilson & Schooler, 1991), the studies by Dane et al. (2012) and Dijkstra et al. (2013) indicate that, for a novice, analytical judgments were more efficient than intuitive judgments. An explanation can be that the participants had experience of the task and thus some level of expertise, whereas the tasks in the latter two studies could be considered more demanding for an undergraduate student who lacks experience. Another observation is that even though the participants' expertise in the studies by Dane et al. (2012) and Dijkstra et al. (2013) can be regarded as being at the lower end of the range, the findings suggest that the effectiveness of using intuition might still be strong in judgmental tasks.

Taken together, these studies suggest that in judgmental tasks the use of intuitive expertise is more efficient than the use of analytical processes. Furthermore, the studies indicate that an analysis can disturb judgments by directing attention away from valuable information to features that are salient and easy to articulate, hence implying that intuitive judgments should be considered before any analytical deliberation takes place. Moreover, these findings have implications for heuristics and biases research. This research largely focuses on analytical tasks with one unequivocal solution. For example, the previously mentioned "the bat and the ball problem" can easily be solved with analytical reasoning. Consequently, for these types of tasks, analytical processes are more efficient to use than intuitive expertise, whereas for judgmental tasks the use of intuitive expertise is better.

4.3 Field studies of intuitive expertise

In this section, we discuss what a selection of field studies[3] can teach us about the use of intuitive expertise, with a particular focus on financial decision-making. The studies are presented chronologically and in groups based on the domain and task studied. The section ends with a concluding discussion about what we can learn from the studies.

The presentation and discussion of each group of studies is structured as follows. First, there is a short overall description of the studies, the participants, and their expertise. Thereafter, findings on the use of intuitive expertise are presented, as well as an analysis drawing on the discussion on dual-process theories. Next, we discuss the environment and other conditions affecting the effectiveness of intuitive expertise. Here, two questions are in focus: First, does the domain lend itself to intuitive expertise? Second, do the tasks lend themselves to the use of intuitive expertise, or would it be more effective to use analytical processes?

4.3.1 The early studies—decision-making by senior managers

Studies in the 1980s and 1990s focused on how senior managers use intuition and analysis in decision-making. These studies describe how intuition is used but do not apply or develop concepts or theoretical frameworks. During that time, a rationalistic, analytical view of decision-making prevailed, and these studies can be seen as a step to counter the predominant rationalistic view by showing how senior managers used intuition. Of these early studies, we have selected three that can be categorized as studying intuitive expertise, that is, Isenberg (1984), Agor (1986), and Burke and Miller (1999). Isenberg (1984) studied how 12 senior managers used intuition. The methods used were in-depth interviews, observations, and think-aloud protocols. Agor (1986) used questionnaires to examine how 200 top managers applied intuition in decision-making, whereas Burke and Miller (1999) interviewed 60 experienced professionals to explore how they used intuition in decision-making. Even though expertise is not discussed in these studies, it is implicitly assumed. Furthermore, the participants in all three studies were senior managers who typically had more than 10 years of experience. Hence, it is reasonable to assume that they had developed expertise in decision-making and that the studies reflect the use of intuitive expertise.

The findings from these studies show that analysis and intuition are used in conjunction. Even though fine-grained data are not available, the studies provide several examples of the use of intuition followed by analysis and vice versa. For example, Isenberg shows a senior manager using intuition to identify a problem that is thereafter analyzed (Isenberg, 1984, p. 85). Another example from Agor (1986, p. 13) describes how an executive starts by analyzing data and thereafter applies intuition for the final judgment.

The studies show that intuition is used in tasks involving people and other judgmental tasks, such as selecting investments. The findings show that these are tasks belonging to the domain of senior managers, lending themselves to expertise. For example, Isenberg describes how successful senior managers spend much of their thoughts on social issues and people: "They try to understand the strengths and weaknesses of others, the relationships that are important to them, what their agendas and priorities are" (Isenberg, 1984, p. 84). Burke and Miller (1999, p. 94) report that 40% of their respondents stated that they use intuition in personnel decisions, for example, in HR (e.g., hiring, training, and performance appraisal). Burke and Miller (1999, p. 94) also provide examples of the use of intuition in judgmental tasks related to financial issues, "such as formulating budgets, estimating prices, and selecting investments." In line with this, Agor (1986, p. 9) describes the use of intuition in investment decision-making as an example of when intuition can play a vital role. Furthermore, Isenberg (1984) shows how senior managers use intuition in problem solving, for example, in identifying problems or testing an analysis.

More than anything, these studies inform us about under what circumstances intuition is used, suggesting that for some tasks, intuition is more effective than the use of analysis. In line with the arguments presented in the previous section, the findings of these early studies suggest that intuition is used in tasks that can be categorized as judgmental. For example, Agor (1986), in his questionnaire-based study, asked managers about when the use of intuition worked best. The answers included (ibid., p. 9):

> *When a high level of uncertainty exists. When little previous precedent exists. When variables are less scientifically predictable. When 'facts' are limited. When facts don't clearly point the way to go. When analytical data are of little use. When several plausible alternative solutions exist to choose from, with good arguments for each. When time is limited and there is pressure to come up with the right answer.*

Consistent with this, Burke and Miller (1999) describe in a concise manner that intuition is used in circumstances of uncertainty and in situations when data are not sufficient.

4.3.2 Studies of decision-making in banks

We have identified two interview-based studies on experts' decision-making in the banking and finance industry. One is conducted by Lipshitz and Schulimovitz (2007), who used interviews with 14 bank loan officers to investigate the use of intuition in credit decisions. The participants had at least 10 years of experience and were responsible for credit services to several clients. Furthermore, the loan officers' salary had a performance-related payment system based on the client's portfolios in the bank. This meant that they received feedback and had a financial incentive to learn their task. Arguably, they can be viewed as having expertise in the domain. The other interview-based study was conducted by Hensman and Sadler-Smith (2011) to explore the use of intuitive expertise in decision-making in a single banking organization. The 15 participants were regarded as experts based on seniority and an average length of experience in the domain of 20 years.

Lipshitz and Schulimovitz (2007) explored challenging credit cases and showed that the interviewees relied on a combination of financial data analysis and intuition. When the financial analysis and intuition were in conflict, the intuitive judgment typically trumped the financial analysis, as described in the following quote (ibid., p. 222):

> *Although loan officers had no objective evidence regarding the validity of these cues and their associated gut feelings, they put more trust in those feelings, in particular their negative gut feelings, than in conflicting financial information. The following assertion by one of the loan officers is representative: "I have a very clear rule: Do not*

> approve a loan, no matter how good its financial information, if you
> have negative vibes about it."

Hensman and Sadler-Smith (2011) asked banking executives to recall
a transaction or case where intuition played a role. As in Lipshitz and
Schulimovitz (2007), the findings show that there is interplay between
intuition and analysis. Intuition could be used to check an analysis
made or vice versa. As illustrated in the quotes below, Hensman and
Sadler-Smith (2011) provide several examples from interviewees showing that intuition is a first step followed by an analysis. This analysis
tests the intuitive judgment. Further, the analysis is used to articulate
and share intuitive judgment with others:

> *I probably rely on gut feel before I do on anything else but it doesn't
> stop me going through the process. The gut feel is there.*
>
> (ibid., p. 56)

> *I suppose it's a bit like in math[s], proving an equation—you're
> doing it back-to-front really—you think you know what result you're
> looking at and you go through the process and determine whether it
> stands up or whether it doesn't.*
>
> (ibid., p. 56)

> *In work I go with my gut instinct but I need to confirm it to so I would
> get some information to confirm what I think is correct . . . because
> I do find in a work environment you can't just make a comment and
> not back it up—you do need to provide somebody with some kind of
> understanding as to why you've come to this conclusion.*
>
> (ibid., p. 58)

Taken together, these two studies show that both intuition and analysis
are considered before a final judgment is made. They also demonstrate
that the use of intuition is related to the outcome of the decision (i.e., performance). The findings of Lipshitz and Schulimovitz (2007) show that
out of the 14 credit assessment cases with negative intuitions, 11 experienced problems afterward. The study by Hensman and Sadler-Smith
(2011) did not explicitly follow up the performance of decision-making.
However, the authors suggest, in line with Lipshitz and Schulimovitz
(2007), that intuition can identify problem areas as illustrated in the
quote: "If something doesn't look right, doesn't smell right, doesn't feel
right—you instantly become wary" (Hensman & Sadler-Smith, 2011,
p. 56). Moreover, Lipshitz and Schulimovitz (2007, p. 221) show how
judgments of material issues can serve as a support in credit judgments:

We visited the plant and it looked well kept, clean, and orderly. The secretary had all the records at hand, and they were well prepared for our visit.

In sum, these studies inform us about under what circumstances intuition is more effective than an analysis. In this respect, the study by Lipshitz and Schulimovitz (2007) is especially interesting. It gives examples of situations when financial analysis and intuition were in conflict, and it shows that in these situations intuitive judgment trumped financial analysis. Hence, this study suggests that intuitive judgments provide additional information and relevant guidance in credit decisions. For example, intuitive judgments included the credibility of the loan applicant, that is, the individual involved in shaping the future of her or his business. Similarly, Hensman and Sadler-Smith (2011, p. 57) describe executives' decision-making as a task that "did not always have a clear right-or-wrong answer; rather they were judgment calls in which intuition had an important role to play."

4.3.3 A study of CEO financial decision-making

The study by Woiceshyn (2009) shows how the CEOs of 19 oil companies reason by having them think out aloud in a financial decision-making scenario. The scenario was designed to be realistic, was developed with the support of industry specialists, and was tested with three top executives in other oil companies. It consisted of three options that the participants should assess and then select from. The options consisted of the following types of investments: technology, geographic expansion, and an acquisition.

Sixteen of the CEOs were categorized as being experts, whereas three were "not-so-effective" thinkers. The selection and categorization were based on the opinion by nine industry experts and a historical record of value creation for the experts and modest or mixed records for the "non-experts." The median industry experience of the experts was 24 years and for the "non-experts" it was 27 years.

When making their decision, the CEOs went back and forth between the use of intuitive expertise and analysis. The iteration continued throughout the whole decision-making process, ending with a commitment to one alternative or a combination of alternatives. A difference between the experts and nonexperts was that the former focused on the essentials, that is, factors influencing the profitability of an oil company, whereas the nonexperts used information that was less relevant for assessing the different options. The finding is in line with the discussion in Section 2.4, that is, that experts see "deep structures" and nonexperts see "surface structures."

Another difference between experts and nonexperts was that the former, although relying on a combination of intuitive expertise and analysis, strived to do their "the homework." They collected as many facts as possible and also consulted others, including outside expert opinion. The nonexperts did not do this to the same extent and were less focused in their thoughts. Moreover, in the paper, the author argues that the findings on the decision-making process of expert CEOs decrease cognitive biases such as overconfidence. Heuristics and biases research shows that bringing in an outside view can mitigate some biases such as overconfidence (see, for example, Kahneman, 2011).

Taken together, these findings show, in line with the studies of decision-making in banks, that both intuition and analysis are considered before any final judgment is made. Hence, in financial decision-making, experts use a combination of intuitive and analytical judgments. Furthermore, the study indirectly supports that financial decision-making lends itself to expertise. The reason is that the expert CEOs had a track record of good performance from both their present oil company and former employers within the same industry. Presumably, financial decision-making constitutes a critical part of their work.

In sum, Woiceshyn (2009) describes financial decision-making as a spiraling process using both analysis and intuition. When judging the options, the CEOs first tried to get an overview and thereafter "zoomed in" on details. Hence, each option seemed to be broken down into different parts. For those parts in which information was available, an analysis could be made; for those parts in which information was not available, or was ambiguous, intuition was used. Taken together, this suggests that financial decision-making encompasses a broad array of issues: some can be supported or solved by analysis whereas in others, intuition is used.

4.3.4 Studies of financial decision-making under extreme uncertainty

The papers by Huang and Pearce (2015) and Huang (2018) report findings from four studies. The paper by Huang and Pearce (2015) includes three studies: an inductive study examining angel investors' decision-making; an experimental study testing the relative importance of intuitive expertise and analysis in decision-making; and an experimental study testing the accuracy of decision-making. The study by Huang (2018) is an inductive study that is based on interviews, observations, and documents.

The three studies in Huang and Pearce (2015) explore early-stage investment decision-making by angel investors. Decision-making of this type is characterized by extreme uncertainty, that is, "they decide on investments in ideas for markets that often do not yet exist, and they propose new products and services without knowing whether they will work" (Huang & Pearce, 2015, p. 636). The studies are based on rich data from interviews, observations of meetings, documents, and experiments. For example, the first study in Huang and Pearce (2015) builds on more than 100 interviews and observations from more than 35 meetings.

Huang and Pearce (2015) found that investors continuously used intuition and analysis in their decision-making. They focused on what the authors describe as perceptions of the entrepreneur and business viability data, for example, information gathered from the business plan presented by the entrepreneur. The investors used intuition in judgments of the founding entrepreneur and to assess business viability data, hence showing how intuition is used in interaction with analysis. The following two quotes from interviews in their study illustrate these two usages of intuition:

> . . . *you notice right away, sometimes within five seconds of meeting the entrepreneur, how you feel about them and what your overall sense is for them as a person.*

> (ibid., p. 644)

> *I need the numbers and the narrative—the business plan makes sense alongside the fellow who wrote the plan, and the fellow will only make sense alongside the business model and the value proposition he thinks is worth offering to me . . . how else do I know how the decision feels . . . whether he's got that unfair advantage or not . . . I may decide later that there's nothing worth a penny in the plan, but that doesn't mean that I don't want to see it and that it doesn't matter in the decision.*

> (ibid., p. 647)

Furthermore, the findings of Huang and Pearce (2015) show that investors' decision-making relied more on perceptions of the entrepreneur than business viability data. Still, collecting and analyzing data about the business was important, as illustrated in the quote below. Thus, even though intuitive judgments of the entrepreneur were determining whether the investor would invest, a thorough analysis was important, similar to what Woiceshyn (2009) found:

I always go through a full due diligence process. . . I check everything out; I put everything into my models. I'm really diligent about collecting bits and pieces; throwing out red herrings. But that only gets you so far . . .

(Huang & Pearce, 2015, p. 643)

Huang (2018) explores financial decision-making in an inductive study of decision-making in early-stage investments. The study shows that investors' decision-making can be described by two process models. The first process starts with an analytical analysis followed by a more intuitively led process, eventually resulting in a self-focused narrative (justification) for making or declining the investment. The other process starts with the intuitive followed by the analytical. Huang suggests that the choice of process is based on the investor's risk stance, that is, whether the investor has a "control-focused" stance (starting with numbers and other data) or a more "choice-based" stance (starting with perceptions of the entrepreneur and the investment opportunity). Ultimately, the process serves as a means to substantiate action. She writes that investors "cognitively and emotionally reframe investment risks into a compelling narrative that transcends avoidance behaviour and leads investors to invest." (Huang, 2018, p. 1821). Huang suggests that decision-making is an elaborate "intuiting process" involving both Type 1 and Type 2 processes, that is, intuitive and analytical processing. She describes it as:

. . . over the course of the intuiting process, investors will weave in numerous interrelated decision factors (economic or financial information and social or behavioral cues) to form premises about investment opportunities.

(Huang, 2018, p. 1840)

Similar to the findings in Huang and Pearce (2015), investors relied a great deal on intuitive judgments of the entrepreneur, as expressed by one of the investors:

It's things like, how committed do they seem. Are they going to go back to their "day-jobs," or is this something that they're really committed to. You get a sense for these things when you spend time with [the entrepreneur] and you listen to how they talk about their company.

(Huang, 2018, p. 1835)

These studies (Huang, 2018; Huang & Pearce, 2015) are especially interesting with respect to domains and tasks lending themselves to expertise, because they show that even in a domain as complex and uncertain as early-stage investments it is possible to acquire expertise in decision-making. This is directly demonstrated in the third study by Huang and Pearce (2015), in which they show that investors' intuitive judgments of the entrepreneur accurately predict the long-term investment profitability. Arguably, as the expert investors in the other studies by Huang and Pearce (2015) and Huang (2018) had been active and survived in the domain for a long period of time, this supports the notion that investment decision-making of early-stage investments is a domain that lends itself to expertise. This also relates to deliberate practice with repetition and feedback, which is accentuated for angel investors. The reason is that they are individual investors who invest their own money, and thus feedback is salient.

Furthermore, the finding that expertise can be developed even in financial decision-making under extreme uncertainty provides support to recent research by Ward and colleagues (Ward et al., 2018, 2020). These researchers argue that a vital part of expertise is about individuals' skilled adaption to change, for example, using knowledge in changing contexts. This is something that early-stage investments provide as each investment has its own unique context, for example, in terms of products, services, and markets.

We can conclude, similar to the banking studies and CEOs' financial decision-making, that both intuitive and analytical judgments are considered before any final judgment is made. This provides additional support for the view that financial decision-making combines intuitive and analytical judgments. However, the studies show that intuitive expertise was especially important in the judgment of the entrepreneur. This task can be described as judgmental, because the capabilities of an entrepreneur are arguably not suitable for analytical processes. It can also be noted that researchers such as Thomas and Lawrence (2018) argue that human behavior is typically difficult to predict. However, it seems that predicting the performance of entrepreneurs, that is, those actually involved in developing and executing the business, is a feasible task for expert investors.

4.3.5 Studies of decision-making in acquisition organizations

Our own studies explore the use of intuitive expertise in financial decision-making (Grant & Nilsson, 2020; Grant et al., 2020). Both studies examine acquisitions and the activities and events leading up to the completion of it. The focus is on the people assigned to make the acquisition, that is, the professional acquisition organization, hence the specialists involved in the day-to-day work with the acquisition project. This includes production of the strategic and financial rationales for making the acquisition, and tasks such as negotiations and due diligence.

In a detailed case study, we examined how strategic and financial rationales for making the acquisition were produced (Grant & Nilsson, 2020). We did this by using 12 interviews and documentation used by the acquirer. Our study shows that people involved had expertise, for example, that they had long experience of the tasks with repetition and feedback. Furthermore, we supported this by following up the outcome of the acquisition, three and a half years after closing of the transaction.

In another study by us, we investigate the use of intuitive expertise in acquisition organizations through interviews with seven professionals (Grant et al., 2020). The participants were regarded as experts. This was based on the professional having at least 15 years of experience in the domain, having reached high positions, and having worked in successful firms that foster learning.

Grant and Nilsson (2020) focuses on the task of producing strategic and financial rationales, for example, judgments of synergy areas and quantification of these. We show that this task is, to a large extent, based on the use of intuitive expertise. However, the finalization of approval documents, where strategic and financial rationales are described, is dominated by analytical reasoning. Hence, the task of producing strategic and financial rationales can be seen as consisting of two parts: one using intuitive expertise and the other using analytical reasoning. However, in these two parts, both intuition and analysis are likely being used, even though one dominates.

Grant et al. (2020) build on Grant and Nilsson (2020) and explore the tasks in which intuitive expertise is used in acquisition processes and the relationship between the use of intuitive expertise and analysis. The findings show that the use of intuitive expertise was especially salient in negotiations and due diligence. Furthermore, the study identifies three patterns in the relationship between the use of intuitive expertise and analysis. First, as in all of the previously described field studies, there was a continuous interplay and use of both intuitive expertise and analysis throughout the acquisition, as illustrated by one of the interviewees:

> The intuitive part sort of massages the data which one has. Somewhere you get a feeling, this feels really good, or [the feeling] that something is wrong. I have to dig deeper into this. Something is not as it should be.

(Grant et al., 2020, p. 48)

Second, analysis was applied to test intuitive judgments, as was found by Woiceshyn (2009). The findings provide several examples of how this analytical testing was done with other people taking part in the project, as illustrated in the quote below:

> *It is an advantage to be several people. Because people see different things, reflect on these in different ways and so on. When you sit down together and discuss how the counterpart has reacted you get a better picture.*
>
> (Grant et al., 2020, p. 48)

Third, and in line with Grant and Nilsson (2020) and Hensman Sadler-Smith (2011), analytical reasoning was used to communicate intuitive judgments and make them measurable. One of the interviewees expressed it in the following way:

> *Can one only be intuitive? No, I don't think so. Because someone needs to judge the intuition so to speak. To assess the intuition, you must create some kind of objective measurable parts.*
>
> (Grant et al., 2020, p. 46)

Furthermore, the study provided examples in which intuitive and analytical judgments were in conflict. As in the studies of credit approvals and decision-making under extreme risk (Huang & Pearce, 2015; Lipshitz & Schulimovitz, 2007), this concerned the intuitive judgments of people. In this case, it was about judging the capabilities of the target management.

In summary, our studies (Grant & Nilsson, 2020; Grant et al., 2020) support financial decision-making as a domain prone to expertise. Grant and Nilsson (2020) show that the production of strategic and financial rationales was, largely, based on judgments using intuitive expertise. Furthermore, we suggest based on the outcome of the acquisition that these judgments were successful. Our studies also provide insights into the effectiveness of intuitive expertise. Grant and Nilsson (2020) show that for the task of assessing acquisitions, for example, identifying future synergies and quantifying them, the use of intuitive expertise was vital. Furthermore, Grant et al. (2020) identify additional examples of the use of intuitive expertise, such as judging whether the target management will stay in the company after the acquisition, or whether they believe in the business plan they present. Arguably, all these tasks can be characterized as judgmental. Furthermore, M&A literature supports the notion that acquisition processes are highly complex and are affected by a myriad of factors (see Grant & Nilsson, 2020).

4.3.6 Conclusions from the review of the field studies

Taken together, the field studies inform us about the use of intuitive expertise in financial decision-making, the interrelations between the use of intuitive expertise and analysis, and the effectiveness of the use of intuitive expertise.

The field studies show that intuitive expertise is used in financial decision-making by decision-makers and by specialists involved in it. Most of the studies examine the use of intuition in decision-making by senior managers. This includes the early studies examining senior managers' use of intuition in decision-making (Agor, 1986; Burke & Miller, 1999; Isenberg, 1984); executive decision-making in banks (Hensman & Sadler-Smith, 2011); and CEOs' decision-making of strategic investments (Woiceshyn, 2009). There are also the studies of financial decision-making under extreme risk, that is, angel investors' decision-making in start-up investments (Huang, 2018; Huang & Pearce, 2015). The studies of decision-making in acquisition organizations (Grant & Nilsson, 2020; Grant et al., 2020) and the study of credit decision-making (Lipshitz & Schulimovitz, 2007) deal with specialists with expertise in more narrow domains, and hence these people are typically not formal decision-makers. However, the specialists are highly influential as they provide formal decision-makers with approval documents and arguments.

The studies also show that financial decision-making is not about the use of either intuitive expertise or analysis. On the contrary, all studies show that financial decision-making is a combination of these two approaches. The studies provide several examples of intuitive judgments followed up and tested by analysis (Grant et al., 2020; Hensman & Sadler-Smith, 2011; Huang, 2018; Huang & Pearce, 2015; Isenberg, 1984; Lipshitz & Schulimovitz, 2007; Woiceshyn, 2009). An example is the use of intuitive expertise to identify problems that are subsequently followed up with an analysis (Grant et al., 2020; Hensman & Sadler-Smith, 2011; Isenberg, 1984; Lipshitz & Schulimovitz, 2007). Furthermore, there were several examples of the use of intuitive expertise to test analytical judgments (Grant et al., 2020; Huang & Pearce, 2015; Lipshitz & Schulimovitz, 2007). An example is the intuitive judgment of entrepreneurs to assess the credibility of their business plans (Huang & Pearce, 2015).

Taken together, these findings strongly suggest that both intuition and analysis are considered before a final judgment or decision is made. Consequently, this supports the parallel-competitive model of dual-process theories, where, as explained in Section 3.3., analytical and intuitive processes work in parallel and interact. When the processes are in conflict, both analytical and intuitive judgments are considered. Consequently, the findings from the field studies speak against the default-interventionist model. This model assumes that the default response is intuitive, typically based on the fact that people are cognitive misers and tend to stick with an intuitive response. A reason for these findings could be the context of financial decision-making (see also Hodgkinson & Sadler-Smith, 2018). This context involves a process that evolves over a long period of time, entailing a myriad of judgments, several people, and organizational structures such as formal decision-making procedures. This is radically different from an experimental setting probing only one judgment or decision. However, financial decision-making in a field setting cannot be studied in the same controlled environment. Hence, we cannot preclude from the field studies that some judgments follow the cognitive miser view, even though the overall picture supports the parallel-competitive model.

Moreover, the field studies show how experts efficiently use intuitive expertise. The character of the tasks is judgmental, and it is suitable for the effective use of intuitive expertise. For example, many tasks could be described as having a high level of uncertainty involving predictions about the future. This includes credit decisions (Lipshitz & Schulimovitz, 2007), investment scenarios (Woiceshyn, 2009), and the identification and quantification of synergy areas in acquisitions (Grant & Nilsson, 2020). Another example of a task with judgmental character is investments in start-ups, a task involving extreme risk (Huang, 2018; Huang & Pearce, 2015). Hence, the field studies fulfill the requirements of effective use of intuitive expertise outlined in the previous two sections.

Further, three of the studies directly followed up the outcome of the use of intuitive expertise and showed that it can lead to an efficient outcome (Grant & Nilsson, 2020; Huang & Pearce, 2015; Lipshitz & Schulimovitz, 2007). Lipshitz and Schulimovitz (2007) showed that the use of intuitive expertise could identify problematic credits. This rested largely on intuitive judgments of the credibility of the loan applicant. Huang and Pearce (2015) demonstrate that intuitive judgments about the entrepreneur accurately predict long-term profitability of the investment. In addition, they validate that the use of intuitive expertise is more efficient than the use of analytical processes for identifying successful early-stage investments. Hence, this reveals that even financial decision-making under extreme risk is prone to the use of intuitive expertise.

Moreover, these two studies (Huang & Pearce, 2015; Lipshitz & Schu-limovitz, 2007) suggest that intuitive judgments about the individuals involved in "shaping" the future, in these cases the loan applicant and the entrepreneur, respectively, are critical in financial decision-making. Our own study provides another example of the effectiveness of the use of intuitive expertise (Grant & Nilsson, 2020). We show that intuitive judgments are effective in assessing synergies in acquisitions.

4.4 Summary

Intuitive expertise combines intuition with expertise and can be seen as the capacity to intuitively "draw on our domain specific knowledge in the form of expertise accumulated in the past" (Sinclair, 2010, p. 382). This means that we use this capacity to make intuitive judgments and decisions. Based on Kahneman and Klein (2009), and knowledge from our previous chapters on expertise and intuition, we describe and expand on three conditions for intuitive expertise, that is, require-ments for the effective use of intuitive expertise.

First, intuitive expertise builds on dual-process theories of thinking. We argue, in contrast to Kahneman and Klein (2009), for a parallel competitive model of dual processes, meaning that analytical think-ing and intuitive thinking interact. Hence, arguably, we do not believe that in professional settings, such as financial decision-making, the cognitive miser view of humans is valid, that is, meaning that we are "lazy" and typically stick to intuitive judgments even if superior ana-lytical judgments are available. This is strongly supported by the field studies, which show that decision-makers and specialists use intuitive expertise and analysis in a recursive manner.

Second, two criteria related to expertise are that the domain and tasks should be benign to expertise, and that people must have an op-portunity to develop expertise. This relates to our detailed discussion in Chapter 2, where we argue that domain and task characteristics should lend themselves to expertise. Thus, we add dynamic aspects of domains and tasks to Kahneman and Klein (2009); for example, as knowledge and tools develop domains and tasks can become more benign to ex-pertise. Regarding the opportunity to develop expertise, we expand and add depth to Kahneman and Klein (2009) in Chapter 2. For example, that expertise requires a long period of deliberate practice, such as the presence of continuously more challenging tasks, repetition, feedback, and gradual refinement. This also relates to the aspect that experts need continuous practice and a will to keep up with new knowledge and tools.

Third, we add to Kahneman and Klein (2009) the condition that the task's character should be suitable for applying intuitive expertise. We suggest that it can be viewed along a continuum, with judgmental tasks at one end and intellective tasks at the other. For judgmental tasks, the use of intuitive expertise is more efficient than that of analytical processes; however, for intellective tasks, analytical processes are preferred. The field studies support this notion by showing that intuitive expertise is effective in tasks that can be categorized as judgmental, encompassing a high level of uncertainty involving predictions about the future. Examples include assessments of credits, investment in acquisitions, and early-stage investments, that is, tasks with a high risk.

Notes

1 See also review by Salas et al. (2010).
2 To describe the structure of the tasks, the terminology of intellective and judgmental tasks of Laughlin (1980) and Laughlin and Ellis (1986) is used. This is also the terminology used by Dane and Pratt (2007). In line with these three papers, the structure of tasks should be viewed along a continuum. At one end are intellective tasks and at the other end are judgmental tasks.

   Intellective tasks "involve a definitive objective criterion of success, within the definitions, rules, operational, and relationships of a particular conceptual system" (Laughlin, 1980, p. 128). Examples of these are, typically, tasks related to words and language, as well as mathematical, chemical, and engineering problems. Another way to describe intellective tasks is that these have a single answer or solution, or that they are decomposable, that is, they can be broken down into subprocesses and be solved analytically (Dane et al., 2012).

   Judgmental tasks "involve political, ethical, aesthetic, or behavioral judgments for which there is no objective criterion or demonstrable solution. On such tasks, the criterion of success is the subjective consensus of group members themselves or the subjective consensus of an external group, such as judges, supervisors, or researchers" (Laughlin, 1980, p. 128). Shapiro and Spence (1997, p. 66) describe these tasks as having "complex underlying relationships, [with] a huge amount of data on many different variables and from many different sources, much of which covaries or is redundant." Examples of these tasks that they provide are investments in R&D and acquisitions.
3 The field studies were selected from an extensive review of field (nonexperimental) studies on intuition. The principle we used in our selection was to include qualitative studies that related to financial decision-making and had participants that could be seen as having expertise. Woiceshyn (2009) was included, even though it is an experimental study. The reason is that it reports from an experiment in a field-based scenario using professional participants.

References

Agor, W. H. (1986). The logic of intuition: How top executives make important decisions. *Organizational Dynamics, 14*(3), 5–18.

Albrechtsen, J. S., Meissner, C. A., & Susa, K. J. (2009). Can intuition improve deception detection performance? *Journal of Experimental Social Psychology*, *45*(4), 1052–1055.

Burke, L. A., & Miller, M. K. (1999). Taking the mystery out of intuitive decision making. *Academy of Management Perspectives*, *13*(4), 91–99.

Dane, E., & Pratt, M. G. (2007). Exploring intuition and its role in managerial decision making. *Academy of Management Review*, *32*(1), 33–54.

Dane, E., Rockmann, K. W., & Pratt, M. G. (2012). When should I trust my gut? Linking domain expertise to intuitive decision-making effectiveness. *Organizational Behavior and Human Decision Processes*, *119*(2), 187–194.

Dijkstra, K. A., van der Pligt, J., & van Kleef, G. A. (2013). Deliberation versus intuition: Decomposing the role of expertise in judgment and decision making. *Journal of Behavioral Decision Making*, *26*(3), 285–294.

Ericsson, K. A. (2006). The influence of experience and deliberate practice on the development of superior expert performance. In Ericsson, K. A., Charness, N., Feltovich, P. J., & Hoffman, R. R. (Eds.). *The Cambridge handbook of expertise and expert performance* (pp. 683–703). New York: Cambridge University Press.

Ericsson, K. A., Charness, N., Hoffman, R. R., & Feltovich, P. J. (Eds.). (2006). *The Cambridge handbook of expertise and expert performance*. New York, NY: Cambridge University Press.

Grant, M., & Nilsson, F. (2020). The production of strategic and financial rationales in capital investments: Judgments based on intuitive expertise. *The British Accounting Review*, *52*(3), 100861.

Grant, M., Nilsson, F., & Nordvall, A. C. (2020). The use of intuitive expertise in acquisition-making: An explorative study. In Sinclair, M. (Ed.), *Handbook of Intuition Research as Practice* (pp. 39–55). Cheltenham: Edward Elgar Publishing.

Hammond, K. R., Hamm, R. M., Grassia, J., & Pearson, T. (1987). Direct comparison of the efficacy of intuitive and analytical cognition in expert judgment. *IEEE Transactions on Systems, Man, and Cybernetics*, *17*(5), 753–770.

Hensman, A., & Sadler-Smith, E. (2011). Intuitive decision making in banking and finance. *European Management Journal*, *29*(1), 51–66.

Hodgkinson, G. P., & Sadler-Smith, E. (2018). The dynamics of intuition and analysis in managerial and organizational decision making. *Academy of Management Perspectives*, *32*(4), 473–492.

Huang, L. (2018). The role of investor gut feel in managing complexity and extreme risk. *Academy of Management Journal*, *61*(5), 1821–1847.

Huang, L., & Pearce, J. L. (2015). Managing the unknowable: The effectiveness of early-stage investor gut feel in entrepreneurial investment decisions. *Administrative Science Quarterly*, *60*(4), 634–670.

Isenberg, D. J. (1984). How senior managers think. *Harvard Business Review*. *62*(6), 81–90.

Kahneman, D. (2011). *Thinking, fast and slow*. New York, NY: Farrar, Straus and Giroux.

Kahneman, D., & Frederick, S. (2002). Representativeness revisited: Attribute substitution in intuitive judgment. In Gilovich, T., Griffin, D.,

& Kahneman, D. (Eds.). *Heuristics and Biases: The Psychology of Intuitive Judgment* (pp. 49–81). New York, NY: Cambridge University Press.

Kahneman, D., & Klein, G. (2009). Conditions for intuitive expertise: A failure to disagree. *American Psychologist, 64*(6), 515–526.

Lane, S. M., & Schooler, J. W. (2004). Skimming the surface: Verbal overshadowing of analogical retrieval. *Psychological Science, 15*(11), 715–719.

Laughlin, P. R. (1980). Social combination processes of cooperative problem-solving groups on verbal intellective tasks. In Fishbein, M. (Ed.). *Progress in Social Psychology* (vol. 1, pp. 127–155). Hillsdale, NJ: Lawrence Erlbaum Associates.

Laughlin, P. R., & Ellis, A. L. (1986). Demonstrability and social combination processes on mathematical intellective tasks. *Journal of Experimental Social Psychology, 22*(3), 177–189.

Lipshitz, R., & Shulimovitz, N. (2007). Intuition and emotion in bank loan officers' credit decisions. *Journal of Cognitive Engineering and Decision Making, 1*(2), 212–233.

McMackin, J., & Slovic, P. (2000). When does explicit justification impair decision making? *Applied Cognitive Psychology: The Official Journal of the Society for Applied Research in Memory and Cognition, 14*(6), 527–541.

Nordgren, L. F., Bos, M. W., & Dijksterhuis, A. (2011). The best of both worlds: Integrating conscious and unconscious thought best solves complex decisions. *Journal of Experimental Social Psychology, 47*(2), 509–511.

Nordgren, L. F., & Dijksterhuis, A. P. (2009). The devil is in the deliberation: Thinking too much reduces preference consistency. *Journal of Consumer Research, 36*(1), 39–46.

Salas, E., Rosen, M. A., & DiazGranados, D. (2010). Expertise-based intuition and decision making in organizations. *Journal of management, 36*(4), 941–973.

Shapiro, S., & Spence, M. T. (1997). Managerial intuition: A conceptual and operational framework. *Business Horizons, 40*(1), 63–69.

Sinclair, M. (2010). Misconceptions about intuition. *Psychological Inquiry, 21*(4), 378–386.

Thomas, R. P., & Lawrence, A. (2018). Assessment of expert performance compared across professional domains. *Journal of Applied Research in Memory and Cognition, 7*(2), 167–176.

Ward, P., Gore, J., Hutton, R., Conway, G. E., & Hoffman, R. R. (2018). Adaptive skill as the conditio sine qua non of expertise. *Journal of Applied Research in Memory and Cognition, 7*(1), 35–50.

Ward, P., Schraagen, J. M., Gore, J., & Roth, E. M. (Eds.). (2020). *The Oxford handbook of expertise.* Oxford: Oxford University Press.

Wilson, T. D., & Schooler, J. W. (1991). Thinking too much: introspection can reduce the quality of preferences and decisions. *Journal of Personality and Social Psychology, 60*(2), 181–192.

Woiceshyn, J. (2009). Lessons from "good minds": How CEOs use intuition, analysis and guiding principles to make strategic decisions. *Long Range Planning, 42*(3), 298–319.

5 The empirical study

This study explores how decision-makers use intuitive expertise, and how they characterize and have developed their expertise. The context is financial decision-making related to acquisitions,[1] which is the same as our previously described studies. Thus, it complements our studies where we examined the use of intuitive expertise by acquisition organizations (Grant & Nilsson, 2020) and specialists (Grant et al., 2020), that is, people influencing financial decision-making. However, this study focuses specifically on the decision-makers.

The empirical study is based on interviews with 12 high-performing senior executives, all of whom possess more than 20 years of experience in senior positions. The interviewees hold—or have held—a CEO position, a CFO position, or a similar senior executive management position (see Appendix B for a more detailed description). Arguably, based on their long experience and senior positions, they can be classified as decision-makers who possess expertise.

In the analysis, the interviews were complemented with additional data from secondary sources such as company websites and business press.[2] This was an iterative process, going back and forth between themes and ideas found in the data, previous research, and the data (see Appendix B for a description of the method). The results of this are the findings presented and discussed in this chapter.

To position the results from the empirical study in relation to the literature review, we use Figure 1.1. As explained in Chapters 1–4, the ellipse to the left in the figure represents "affectively charged judgments that arise through rapid, nonconscious, and holistic associations" (Dane & Pratt, 2007, p. 40), resulting in *intuition*. The ellipse to the right in the figure represents *expertise*, that is, "consistently superior performance on a specified set of representative tasks" (Ericsson & Lehman, 1996, p. 277). The shaded area in the figure represents *intuitive expertise* or,

DOI: 10.4324/9781003035725-5

in other words, how experts use intuition when making judgments and decisions (Kahneman & Klein, 2009).

The findings show that intuitive expertise is used by decision-makers together with visible and structured analysis. Hence, decision-making is not about using either intuition or analysis but rather an interplay between them. However, the findings show that in financial decision-making intuition often plays a decisive role. One reason is that it concerns judgmental tasks involving uncertainties and/or ambiguities. Not surprisingly, decision-makers are well aware of the large ambiguities and uncertainties that are inherent in most financial decision-making and especially in acquisitions. Moreover, the expertise that senior executives use when making these decisions can be related to two distinct areas: strategic and operational expertise and M&A expertise. Arguably, having expertise in these areas could be seen as a prerequisite for successful financial decision-making. Furthermore, the findings pave the way for discussing the effectiveness of intuitive expertise. This is illustrated in Figure 5.1.

Starting on the left-hand side of the figure (the ellipse denoted *intuition*), interviewees provided some examples of financial decisions in M&A with poor outcomes. Overconfidence, or lack of expertise, was fairly salient in several of these. Hence, the senior executives seemed to rely on intuition without having the required expertise. Moving over to the area of *intuitive expertise* (the shaded area in the figure), findings show examples of overreliance on analysis and too little reliance

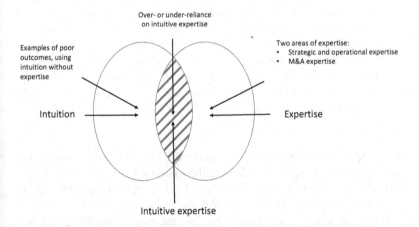

Figure 5.1 Effectiveness of intuitive expertise (see also Figure 1.1., adapted from Salas et al., 2010, p. 945).

on intuitive expertise. However, there were also indications of too much reliance on intuitive expertise without sufficient analysis being made. Finally, illustrated by the right-hand side of the figure (the ellipse denoted *expertise*), we identified two areas of expertise required in financial decision-making. The findings show that both of them are prerequisites for effective intuitive expertise, as explained above. Consequently, lack of expertise in one of the areas can lead to poor outcomes of financial decision-making.

In the following sections the findings are presented and discussed in detail. The overall conclusions, and how they relate to current knowledge in the area, will be presented in the final chapter of the book. The final chapter will also discuss ideas for future research.

5.1 The characteristics of intuitive expertise

When we asked interviewees what characterizes an expert in financial decision-making, a common theme in their answers was the importance of long experience. One interviewee, as quoted below, expressed it as participating in many acquisitions. That experience will contribute toward building knowledge about what works and what does not, in other words what is important. The quote captures well responses from other interviewees, also stressing the significance of practical hands-on experience and the experiences of misjudgments and failures:

> *I actually believe that it is . . . to have been part of it. To have experience of what can go wrong. There are few things that look as easy on paper as creating value after an acquisition. [. . .] we have figures on a paper and we say—this looks great! And all those things that will not make it happen in the end. . . they are usually very difficult to express. We know that a lot of all this is about people and how you get them on board. It is about leadership, methods and the experience of the people who will make it happen. That is difficult to express.*
>
> (B)[3]

Also apparent in the interviews was the difficulty of disentangling the characteristics of expertise in financial decision-making. The reason can probably be found in the tacit nature of expertise. Polanyi (2009, p. 4) described it in the famous quote: "We can know more than we can tell."

When we analyzed the interviews further, as well as other data, we identified several patterns related to the understanding of expertise in financial decision-making. First, we noted some general characteristics of how expertise is developed. Second, we identified two areas of expertise in financial decision-making within M&A. The areas are strategic and operational expertise, and M&A expertise. There were several examples of how lack of expertise in these areas had led to poor outcomes. Arguably, having expertise in both of these areas is a prerequisite for successful financial decision-making of M&As. We will discuss this finding further in the last section of the chapter.

Moreover, the backgrounds of the interviewees differed. Several had multiple industry expertise; others had only expertise in M&A, or from one single industry and in M&A. Notably, expertise in M&A financial decision-making could not be related to only one of the areas identified. Therefore, as argued above, it is essential for the outcome that the decision-makers together cover both areas of expertise identified and necessary in financial decision-making. One of the interviewees explained:

> *In the composition of the board, it is very important that you have different qualities and different backgrounds so that you get a thorough analysis.*

(G)

5.2 The development of intuitive expertise

In the interviews and archival data, it is possible to discern some general patterns of how intuitive expertise is developed. It seems like this development is related to having long and rich experience as well as exposure to challenges. A salient pattern that almost all interviewees described was learning by making your own mistakes. An example of how this can be made possible is by being part of an organization that allows mistakes. Another more surprising example is quotes about managers who even consciously allow mistakes for the sake of learning. Generally, the development of expertise was described as something that took place gradually. Hence, interviewees had difficulties pinpointing it in any detail. As one of the interviewees expressed it:

> *So, I think there is probably a lot of development that had happened during the years but without being able to say exactly—that hey, this changed, but it's an evolution about learning about things.*

(E)

Other interviewees described their own development when, early on in their career, they started by working hands-on to learn their trade, for example in operations, accounting, or credit assessment. That development was sometimes described in terms such as "starting in the salt-mines" or doing "military duty." In addition, several interviewees mentioned being given challenging tasks or positions at an early age. An example is from one of the CFOs, who described that in a network consisting of 12 CFOs in large industrial companies, an exercise was conducted in which they were asked to identify an important moment in their career. A common experience was that all of them had been given a demanding assignment or position at an early stage of their career. This experience was described to us in the following way:

> *It turned out that the twelve of us had exactly the same experience; that early in your career—you were around 30 years old or something like that—you got an assignment or a position that you basically could not handle. You got a very difficult assignment as a manager, project leader, or whatever. You got coaching from your boss, who were there in the background, but you had to "walk the plank" yourself to check if you could swim or not. All of us had this experience, and we all managed to handle it.*

(F)

In line with this, other interviewees provided examples of difficult situations that challenged their knowledge and experience. It could be how they struggled with a certain unfamiliar task or a new position, both of which had been an important driver in developing their expertise. One interviewee described how, at an early stage of his career, he had been heavily involved in starting up a telecom operator in Brazil. Another interviewee described it as a "difficult school" when he at the time of the IT boom entered the telecom industry as CFO. At the turn of the millennium, times were challenging since the telecom industry was going through major technological and regulatory changes. He described it in the following way:

> *At that time I entered a world that I didn't understand at all. You know there were P/E ratios of 250 and people where buying assets for a billion, that had no profit and cashflows. And it was a totally crazy world. And of course, the size of everything, the size of the assets that we all looked into where so different from that I had been used to. So that was one world and the amount of transactions, kind of first buying everything that was available and then selling everything because you had to, and then the merger, and the integration of the businesses. So, it was a very rich world from the experience point of view. And I used to*

think that during four years' time I was involved in more transactions than any senior partner at Goldman Sachs most likely.[. . .] but that was interesting and of course there you learn to be humble also in that way that many of us, most of us, did wrong decisions, a lot of them.

(E)

A salient element in the development of expertise in M&A financial decision-making was the experience of having made mistakes or taking part in a process in which mistakes were made. Several interviewees describe this as a prerequisite to develop expertise. The experiences of making mistakes also helped them when their careers advanced further. One interviewee even considered making mistakes and learning from them as an "investment":

It is clear that I have made some mistakes when making investments, I am convinced of that. I am sure. But it is also true that to become a manager you should have done some mistakes earlier in your career. You have made mistakes with small sums. You have learnt something. And it is often so that if you have made a mistake and you understand why it went wrong, it is actually an investment.

(J)

Another interviewee pointed out that he was lucky to have managers who believed in him and let him make mistakes. However, in line with other interviewees, the mistakes were limited in scope and did not exceed reasonable bounds:

I had the luck to have . . . many good managers that believed in me and let me make mistakes, and . . . at the same time I had the ability to learn a lot from these mistakes so that I did not have to repeat them too many times.

(C)

That managers let people make mistakes as a way to learn was visible in other interviews as well. One example is a highly successful CEO of a serial acquirer. The CFO described how the CEO challenged the manager responsible for the acquisition by asking detailed questions. Afterward, he approved the acquisition even though he knew that it would likely fail. This suggests that individuals need to accept responsibility and rely on their own judgments even though this can lead to mistakes. What is important is that if it turns out that the acquisition was a mistake, both the individual and the organization must learn from it and, by doing so, develop their intuitive expertise. The CFO described one of these situations in the following way:

> *Then after it was all over [the questioning] he [the CEO] could say: I don't really believe in this. No? OK but why did you approve it then? Well, you know, they must be allowed to make their own mistakes.*
>
> (F)

The CFO continued with a reflection on this type of behavior and the reasons for it:

> *He was well aware that sometimes things go down the drain and therefore he approved investments that he was pretty sure would not work out well. Well thought out, do it and you will learn and you can use it next time. And next time would come quickly since he [the CEO] wanted a lot of action all the time. So next time you will have this experience intuitively.*
>
> (F)

The importance of reflection and learning from failures and successes was brought up by other interviewees as well. One of them expressed, in the quote below, that the gut feeling in M&A financial decision-making is developed by making mistakes and reflecting on them, preferably by listening to other peoples' views on the matter:

> *How do you develop that gut feeling? Well, unfortunately by failing a couple of times. I believe that what is very important—both when you succeed and when you fail—is to reflect on why did we fail and why did we succeed? Why did it go down the drain? What should we have done differently? And sometimes you ask yourself: why did I not raise my hand more or longer when I actually did? And sometimes it is very important to get in other people and perspectives to look at it.*
>
> (G)

5.3 The use of intuitive expertise

The use of intuitive expertise in combination with an analysis based on, for example, formal documents presented or sent to decision-makers, was a prerequisite in financial decision-making. The interviews showed that the strategic reasons for an acquisition were an important starting point. Thereafter, more judgmental tasks came into play, such as making financial forecasts and trying to assess whether the acquirer and the target would be able to work together. In these judgmental tasks, intuitive expertise played a significant role. Furthermore, as some interviewees described it, the use of gut feeling seemed to be important for decision-making, perhaps more so than the financial analysis. One of the CFOs explained in some detail how intuitive expertise was used in some of the acquisitions they had been involved in:

> *I would like to see a write-up, or like an equity story. Why are we doing this? How does it fit into our strategy? What does the logic look like? What are the driving forces but also what does the calculation look like for us? Then I think it's good asking those questions and verifying those questions but also getting a feel for, who are the other party, what are their driving forces, how does this feel? How do we experience their culture when we meet and will we be able to work together? [. . .] I mean, remarkably often it has been the case that the calculation says yes and the gut feeling says no. And unfortunately, it is when the gut feeling says no that it actually fails, even if the calculation looks good.*
>
> (G)

As in the example above, a former CFO with a rich experience from acquisitions, describes his reasoning during the assessment of one of them. He started, in line with the interviewee above, with decision documents including a structured presentation and analysis of the strategy. Thereafter, judgments based on intuitive expertise were made, including, for example, the valuation of the target, the target business plan, and target company management. He explained how he used intuitive expertise in the following way:

> *[first discuss strategy, strategic reason] especially the area like synergies then you start moving more towards intuition and judgment calls, rather than facts. Doing the DCF-based[4] evaluation is the same thing. You can have the facts, somebody has prepared plans and you can do DCFs based on those, but then you need to do your own judgment calls that you know... does it make sense? Is it realistic? [. . .] So, judgment always plays an important role in everything.*
>
> (E)

*... if you have many years behind you and have made a lot of trans-
actions, you get a feeling. You get a feeling from the management
meetings, talking with people and looking into numbers, looking into
history and so on. So, I guess this was a long answer to say that—it
will always be a combination of the technical expertise plus the intuition, the judgment calls, and trying to understand what kind of entity
you really are looking into.*

(E)

An observation from the interviews, perhaps not surprising, was that
the use of intuitive expertise in M&A financial decision-making was
not done without having facts and an explicit analysis available. This
was especially salient for larger or more unusual acquisitions, as illustrated by the interviewee below:

*Actually, I think the gut feeling is present in all acquisitions, it's just
a question of where in the process it hits, when I think about it. Because it's just that I think you require more fundamentals, more discussions to feel comfortable . . . the more unusual the acquisition is
in relation to the company.*

(A)

In the following two subsections, we will discuss in more detail the use
of intuitive expertise. The first section covers findings related to the
extent to which the interviewees relied on intuitive expertise. The following section provides examples of tasks for which judgments based
on intuitive expertise were used.

5.3.1 Reliance on intuitive expertise

All interviewees described that they relied on intuitive expertise in
judgments that proceed financial decision-making. One exception to
this was a CFO of a serial acquirer who emphasized analysis and experience more than intuitive expertise. However, when discussing a large
acquisition, which was much less common, he described that he relied
more on intuitive expertise. Furthermore, the use of intuitive expertise
was not surprisingly, and as shown by evidence from all interviewees,
related to experience. However, there were also examples of over- and
underreliance on intuitive expertise where they should have done more
analysis, or in contrast to that relied more on their intuition. Several

interviewees described that because of their rich experience, they had the confidence to use and rely on intuitive expertise. One of the interviewees described this type of reliance in the following way:

> ... the answer is probably actually almost every time [. . .] because the more experienced you become, the more expert knowledge you have, the more you dare to use your gut feeling.
>
> (D)

Some interviewees stated that intuitive expertise was decisive for the outcome of the acquisition, illustrated in the two quotes below. Hence, these two interviewees were arguing that intuitive expertise trumped analysis when they showed conflicting directions. Other interviewees provided, in line with this, examples of financial decision-making where they should have relied more on their gut feeling:

> And I must say that in many situations, my gut feeling has helped me a lot. It's that, this does not feel right. If I look at the times I regret my decisions and many of them concern personnel [then I should have relied on my gut-feel].
>
> (J)

> No, what happens in that situation is that the gut feeling says no and I have so far never made a good deal when the gut feeling says no and the head says yes. You get. . . . And yes, in principle it has usually gone well, even if it has been the other way around that the gut feeling says yes, but the head says no. I have learned to listen to the gut feeling quite a lot.
>
> (C)

One of the interviewees, whom we met with several times, had taken time to reflect in depth about how he, as CFO and currently as a board member, used intuition in judgment and decision-making and what role it played. He characterized himself as an intuitive decision-maker. He even suggested, as shown in the following quote, that the use of intuitive expertise is a prerequisite or characteristic of people reaching high managerial positions.

> But I think . . . it is easier for those who have the ability to make intuitive decisions and do it with some accuracy to reach high positions . . . When I think of my colleagues in the management at company X or for that matter the group management in company Y, which I was

close to, it was still mainly people who were relatively quick in their decision-making and in their assessments.

(K)

However, a reflection he made was that sometimes he was too fast, not considering or evaluating the facts that were available. Explanations for this could be overconfidence or misjudgment of the importance of some facts. He explains:

Then it was probably almost always the case that it was because it went a little too fast. That is, in the sense that it went a little too fast, while there were facts available . . . that I missed or that I did not value correctly or that I underestimated the importance of.

(K)

5.3.2 Judgmental tasks

The interviews showed that judgments, based on intuitive expertise, were related to areas of ambiguities. To a large extent, these ambiguities were related to judging what would likely happen in the future. In an M&A context, financial decision-making will typically revolve around ambiguities related to questions such as: Do we believe in the sales forecast of the target? How motivated is the target company management to continue develop their business? Will we be able to integrate the target company? Will we be able to realize the synergy potential?

Another salient pattern that could be observed in the interviews was that the use of intuitive expertise related to two overall categories of judgments. The first category is judgments needed in the construction of strategic and financial rationales (Grant and Nilsson, 2021). These rationales are made visible in decision documents that include financial forecasts, valuation, synergies, and integration plans. The second category is judgments that are made to assess people (e.g., managers) and their capabilities. These types of judgments are hardly ever to be found in decision documents.

The interviewees described many of the ambiguities that surface when constructing the rationales presented in decision documents. There seemed to be awareness among all interviewees that decision documents only show one of many possible scenarios. Interviewees expressed this uncertainty in statements such as "there are so many uncertain factors" or "nobody knows about the future anyway." Uncertainty was further accentuated when new technologies were involved. In those cases, judgments of the individuals in target companies, and whether they would be able to work together and achieve what they had envisioned, were critical. The quote below is an illustration of such judgments:

> *New technologies [. . .] should the business case look good, half good or look bad? It's just a matter of changing the assumptions. That's what you think in five years' time and so on. Then, what matters most is . . . what do we believe ourselves as a company and what do these individuals that should work together believe, and can we work together as team to achieve this?*
>
> (G)

Unsurprisingly, the interviewees were well aware of the uncertainties that characterize financial forecasts, synergies, and valuation with their underlying assumptions. As one of the interviewees expressed in the quote below, the numbers can show what you want them to show. Therefore, intuitive expertise was necessary to use when judging whether the financial numbers and assumptions were realistic and made sense:

> *But then when it comes to being able to decide, then I do my thing, my view of it. This is not something that is directly visible, but I do my own judgment what I think. That's kind of a way to count and. . . . I put in my own belief then. Is it go or no go. The numbers you can show this and that then, what you want as well.*
>
> (B)

> *[Structured analysis] And then you have to do it, how likely is it? That it will be like this. The gut feeling then, will it succeed like this, and what are the risks and what are . . . the pitfalls. What does it boil down to?*
>
> (B)

The other category of ambiguities concerned judgments of people in the acquirer and target companies. All interviewees described this as critical in M&A financial decision-making. It was described as more important than the company valuation, which was considered to be a "hygiene factor." As one of the interviewees described it:

> *For me, it is more it [the strategy and people] that decides, rather than the valuation and analysis itself. That is what makes it a good or a bad acquisition. It is not if you have calculated NPV correctly, or if all*

possible risk scenarios have been taken into account etc. It is of course important to know the risks, but crucial for my judgment if it will be a good or a bad investment is if it fits strategically, if we have knowledge and can integrate it, and if we have the right people on board—in our company and in the target—to turn it into something really good.

(D)

Similarly, one of the interviewees who worked for private equity companies described that having a management team with strong capabilities and expertise was a prerequisite for any investment made. The reason, as described in the quote above, is that people in the acquirer and target need to have the ability to turn it into a successful acquisition. Hence, as financial decision-making concerns the future, there are, obviously, large uncertainties as to how it will turn out. However, having the right people is something that will influence and shape the future and outcome of an acquisition. This is something that decision-makers can influence, in contrast to, for example, environmental changes, such as overall market developments. At the same time, the judgment of people was characterized as an area of uncertainty. One of the interviewees characterized this as an area where facts will not always provide all answers:

And looking at this transaction you need to test the management and test yourself. That whatever the figures show, can we manage this? Will we ever be able to take it over? Will we ever be able to integrate it? And you know in these areas you do face situations where facts don't give you all the answer.

(E)

An important judgment concerned the manager who will have the business responsibility for the acquired company. Several interviewees mentioned the critical importance of this judgment and especially how the manager plans to integrate the acquirer and target. As described below, this included meeting and listening to the manager:

In general, in boards, we often ask to meet . . . especially when there are large acquisitions, to meet the person who will actually take care of it. That is, the business area manager or whoever it is, because that's where it's going to happen. So that one feels that it actually is their acquisition. Because for me it's very much about integration [. . .] you often hear in the voice how people present if they say—this is what I believe in.

(A)

An aspect of people assessment that was mentioned as critical by several interviewees was whether management would be able to manage cultural differences. Thus, part of the assessment also included evaluating and comparing the culture of the acquirer and the target. One of the interviewees described, in line with other interviewees, that he made this assessment largely based on gut feeling or intuition:

> *When you meet people, you feel if you will be able to work together. Will we be able to agree and compromise or will there be frictions? So, it's definitely an important issue once you look at the analysis and see that there's a logic. This makes sense, this is a pretty good calculation. At this point the gut feeling that you describe is important. But I would say that the gut feeling is perhaps more important in regards to the people who are going to do the job on both ends.*
>
> (G)

Apart from specific areas of ambiguities, interviewees described that they used their intuitive expertise for an overall judgment of the acquisition. One of the interviewees, as quoted below, described this judgment in terms of risk, especially the risk that the acquisition will not succeed:

> *People become an aspect of that. And what are people like and what does the culture look like . . . how motivated do we seem and . . . what have I kind of learned, how difficult is it actually? And then there will be something that looks decently scientific, but which is not. Just when it comes to risk . . . what to say? The risk factor of that. Yes.*
>
> (B)

5.4 Areas of expertise

In the introduction to the chapter, we pointed out that we have found two distinct areas of expertise in financial decision-making: strategic and operational expertise, and M&A expertise. These areas are discussed below.

5.4.1 Strategic and operational expertise

Strategic and operational expertise was described by several interviewees as being a critical proficiency in M&A financial decision-making. Interviewees emphasized the requirement of having long experience in an industry in order to obtain the expertise necessary to make strategic and operational judgments. Perhaps that standpoint was not surprising considering that all of the interviewees had at least 20 years of experience from one type of industry or in adjacent industries.

One CFO with a long experience in a highly acquisitive company described strategic expertise as a cornerstone for financial decision-making. Hence, this points out at how strategy is the base for assessing the value and integration of the target:

> *The valuation of how the acquisition will be, if it is interesting, if it is properly priced, how we should be able to be a better owner than the current owner. It all boils down to the fact that you are highly confident that you have a very clear strategy.*

(L)

Two examples of how strategic and operational expertise was expressed are described below. Even though one interviewee had experience from the pulp and paper industry and the other from banking, they expressed expertise in a similar way. However, the interviewee from the banking industry described, at the same time, skepticism to judgments such as this, and mentioned examples where a deeper analysis had shown a different picture, hence pointing to the risk of overconfidence and lack of analysis:

> *[in this industry] I can walk into the factory almost half-blind and tell how it should look.*

(J)

> *I have visited 350 bank branches or 400 or whatever it is. Surely, I do not have to be, or needed at that time to be in a bank branch for a very long time before I understood whether it was well managed or not.*

(K)

It should be noted, however, that having knowledge about an industry does not always lead to strategic or operational expertise. One of the interviewees stressed that senior executives in a company can be knowledgeable of an industry but still not possess expertise. Hence, they do not necessarily have deep strategic or operational knowledge. They may be able to talk about the industry but lack deeper insights. Another example, similar to this line of reasoning, is from an interviewee describing that the company had insights into how the industry and products would develop. Unfortunately, they lacked the necessary strategic and operational expertise to develop their products in that direction. He expressed it as follows:

We knew it was going to be a [certain product]. But we didn't have the ability to do it ourselves. We had the product in pictures, we saw how everything would work together. We had even seen that five years ago. But we didn't have the ability to get there. And then we come back to these experts and people. Maybe we didn't even know how to ask the question to get to where we wanted.

(J)

Interviewees also provided examples of failed acquisitions based on the decision-makers' lack of strategic and operational expertise. One example was a large company in the IT industry that wanted to make an acquisition in an adjacent industry. Even though the company and their senior executives possessed some knowledge about the industry, they did not have enough operational expertise to sufficiently question and assess the target. It later turned out that the acquired company did not have the expertise and capabilities anticipated. The acquisition was a disappointment. Another example was a bank moving into an adjacent business. Similar to the previous example, the decision-makers lacked operational expertise and the acquisition turned out to be a failure in the end. An additional explanation for the bad outcome could probably be attributed to overconfidence, as the previous acquisition by the bank had turned out to be a success. The interviewee expressed it in the following way:

[In the second acquisition] we started from the wrong premise. Just because the former [acquisition] went well, the next one doesn't have to go well also. We weren't really prepared for it, and it was an industry that we really did not understand in depth ourselves. So, the decision-makers did not have the necessary knowledge [of the adjacent business.]

(H)

The difficulty of financial decision-making in industries where strategic and operational expertise was lacking was mentioned by several interviewees. Still, examples of successful acquisitions in new industries were also provided. Companies that succeeded seem to have allowed a longer time, up to several years, to learn more about the new industry in general and the targets in particular. The company could also test and learn by making a small acquisition, and, pending the outcome, thereafter make a larger entry into the industry.

Investments in new technologies were described by several interviewees as being especially difficult. Because technologies could be emerging or changing fast, few, if any, experts would exist. Moreover, the technologies and the operational expertise needed to evaluate it could be very narrow, and thus few experts could be found. A strategy to manage this was to make several smaller acquisitions and treat these more as outsourced R&D. One of the interviewees expressed it in the following way:

> *That's why high-tech acquisitions usually fail. If you don't do it the way they do it in Silicon Valley. . . . You buy smaller companies all the time. It's nothing short of outsourced R&D.*

(J)

In industries such as high-tech and consultancy, expertise and the value of the companies largely reside in individuals. The risk is that these individuals will leave the company after the acquisition is done. Therefore, the integration of the target is of critical importance:

> *[In consultancy company A] there is a risk that people will quit. You buy people, to be honest. And then you ask yourself—what are the chances that people will stay? Otherwise, you will buy an empty company. And how should you integrate? I think the cultural issues have always been underestimated, but they become even more important when buying professionals... individuals, i.e., consultancy companies if you call it that. Because if the culture doesn't work, the asset walks away, it disappears (laughs). Then it doesn't matter which position you have on the market because suddenly you have nothing.*

(A)

5.4.2 *M&A expertise*

Expertise in M&A was, not surprisingly, described by the interviewees as an important area in financial decision-making. This area of expertise covers the whole M&A process, from strategy and acquisition-making (initiation, due diligence, negotiations, and closing) to the integration of the acquired company. Most of the interviewees had many years of experience from working in highly acquisitive companies. Some had worked as advisers or CFOs playing an active role in large acquisitions, less so of handling smaller ones. Others had gained their M&A experience from being a member of the management team and / or the board.

Apart from more general M&A expertise, interviewees provided examples of the different areas they particularly focused on and had obtained expertise from. These were to be found in both acquisition-making and integration. Another area, covering all M&A topics, was the development of an M&A capability.

The two interviewees who had worked as advisers and were experts in some or all parts of the acquisition-making process provided examples of the tasks related to their specific experience of M&A financial decision-making. Examples of these tasks are how to structure due diligence work, valuation and valuation modeling, synergy estimations, and capital-market aspects of an acquisition. One of the interviewees described how she became an expert in M&A after having made numerous due diligences, and how this expertise was used by the board when assessing acquisitions:

> *I'm very sure what questions to ask and what it should look like . . . ,*
> *the process around it and that the digging is deep enough.*

(B)

Another interviewee stressed the importance of discussing how much the company is willing to pay the so-called "walk-away price." Based on earlier experience, this interviewee considered that type of discussion and decision to be very difficult, as expressed in the quote:

> *Then I think what is very important when you look into an acquisition*
> *is that you set certain ranges and limits—how far can you go? How*
> *much are you really willing to pay? And when it goes over that price*
> *you need to walk away. And that's difficult. That's difficult because*
> *many times you have been spending many hours and a lot of resources*
> *and you are very enthusiastic about it and you kind of have promised*
> *your board already that—Hey we will make this happen, and then*
> *you will need to say no, let's not do it. And that is a tough call.*

(E)

One of the interviewees emphasized the significance of having a well-motivated management team to be able to handle the many challenges that are common during the integration phase. Another interviewee with long experience of integration—both in operational roles and in boards of highly acquisitive companies—expressed how she spent a lot of time trying to understand how the acquired company would be integrated. She also stressed the importance of following up the outcome of the integration and to learn from it:

> *I have a tendency asking questions like: If we buy this how are you*
> *going to take care of it? Otherwise, if you do not know to handle it,*

the acquisition calculation will completely wrong. So, I spend a lot of time understanding how do we intend to integrate this? And then we also get a follow-up on whether this went well. So, it's not just a follow-up that's financial, it is also that integration worked well.

(A)

The cultural aspect was raised by several interviewees. This concerned understanding the culture in the acquirer and target company and how they would fit together. This also depended on how the target would be integrated. One of the interviewees described it as follows:

I have been even more interested over the years in cultural values in companies that we are going to acquire, versus the culture we have ourselves. Because I believe there are so many acquisitions that haven't worked out as planned. On the surface it can sound great, but there can be two completely different cultures that are clashing with each other. . . . But it also depends on how the company is organized, how the stand-alone acquisition should be arranged. . . . For companies where it will be integrated quickly, cultural values become hugely important.

(A)

Examples of poor outcomes of acquisitions, due to incompatible cultures, were also provided. Among these were not only large mergers but also the difficulty and substantial risk when a large company acquires a small technology company or a start-up. One of the CFOs recognized that this was a common problem discussed among CFOs of large companies. The risk that a large company "suffocates" a small target was described in the following way:

I have been involved in buying companies, great companies, but you have felt: Yes 20 good innovators, that is fine, but should they be managed by a large company? Should they enter that world? Is that going to work really? Are we going to suffocate them? How do we not suffocate them and so on? And then, remarkably often, it doesn't work either. Then it's just a matter of taking control and try to keep the individuals that you need to be kept and still making this fly.

(G)

I've talked to a lot of CFOs and this is a huge problem. When we come and present our governance model and things like that, especially when we do acquisition of technology companies—things that are more innovative, like start-ups—there's a huge risk that we'll just kill them and lose it.

(G)

5.5 Articulating intuition and social dynamics

The interviewees gave several examples of how intuition is articulated. One example of this is the use of explicit analysis not only to display intuition in analytical terms, but also to test intuition. We also found many examples of how social dynamics affected the use of intuition. Even though this was not the focus of the study, there are reasons to believe that social dynamics are important in how intuition is articulated and used in financial decision-making. In the following two subsections, we will discuss findings related to the articulation of intuition and social dynamics.

5.5.1 Articulating intuition

The quote below illustrates how an explicit analysis was used to articulate and test intuition. It describes how an interviewee, before finally concluding that he should rely on his intuition, reflected on whether all available information had been thoroughly analyzed:

> *Before you reach a conclusion, you still think about if I can trust my gut feeling this time or is there something I should analyse more closely. So maybe you reach the conclusion that; no, I feel safe. There are no facts that I have ignored and so you go, and then you make your decision. [. . .] when I made intuitive decisions, there was still a moment of reflection always in [. . .] this assessment as I did.*

(K)

As illustrated below, an explicit analysis was also used to formulate and understand intuition, what we have chosen to call "articulating the intuition." This form of articulation could also be interpreted as a way to "make sense" of the intuition (see, for example, Weick, 1995):

> *And what I'm trying to think that's why I . . . and just formulate what it is that makes that – what is it that I really see? Trying to formulate it for myself. Why does my feeling come? Because I think it is important then to try, what is it really? And formulate . . . that way then.*

(B)

Another interviewee stated that he needed time to make the intuition more concrete, or, in other words, to articulate it for himself:

> *And it's probably only when I see numbers or conclusions that go against what my gut feeling says that I have to break it down and make it logical for myself, and it usually takes 24 hours for me to get there. I can say, no, no. I cannot figure out why in a meeting, but it takes quite a long time for me to figure that out.*

(C)

The following two quotes illustrate not only how intuition could be articulated in more general terms but also how arguments found in decision documents could be used. Several interviewees described board discussions in similar ways, that is, expressing their intuition using rather vague expressions such as "this will be easy for us."

> *When I explain [at a board meeting]. . . I do not express myself precisely in numbers. When I justify my position I talk more like, this is how I think, I think this is difficult and I think this will be easy for us. And in the end, I think it's worth doing this? Because I think we will surpass this value or yes, whatever it may be.*

(B)

> *And then it is often that you find . . . in the set of facts, what you want. And if I have a very negative feeling from the beginning . . . then I look more critically [. . .] And trying to find, what could it be that does not still fly. [. . .] it becomes more of such an aspect than if from the beginning I think this is positive . . . the angle will be different, because there is something from the beginning that is positive or negative.*

(B)

Interviewees also gave examples of when the intuition said "no." However, interviewees not being able to display the intuition in analytical terms made it difficult for it to be used in financial decision-making. The following quote illustrates such a situation. It shows how a CFO could not articulate his intuition and because of that he felt that his arguments against a large acquisition were too weak. It turned out later that the acquisition was a failure:

> *I think that was a transaction where I didn't feel happy about it, but I had no solid data saying that it was a wrong decision, it was just a feeling.*

(E)

In line with the example above, a board member described how he in-tuitively knew that the company business model was wrong. However, he could not describe why. He said:

> *Does [company X] have the right business model? No, absolutely not, I said. No, what should it look like then? Yes, I do not know, but if the business model was right then it would not look like this. [. . .] There you can say that there I knew, or intuitively I was completely clear to myself that this is completely wrong. But I could not really describe how we would get back on track.*
>
> (I)

5.5.2 Intuition and social dynamics

Interviewees gave several examples of social dynamics, hindering or holding back their use of intuition. One example was a situation in which the other group members have different opinions regarding a possible acquisition. Discussions such as these could also be affected by the social dynamics that follow from the hierarchical structure of companies or the relationship between the board and the management of the company. The example below shows how a CFO could be hesi-tant to use his intuition if a lot of opposition was expected, for exam-ple, if he was the only one who had a divergent view:

> *That is, when you really think about it objectively, is this the right decision or the wrong decision? Should I say no even though I am about to say yes? And then you feel that yes, there is a lot to suggest that I should say no. But in that case, it's going to stir things up. I will get a lot of opposition, it will be a very unpopular decision, I am almost alone in this meeting feeling this hesitation, and I certainly have a strong position in the meeting. But not so strong that I would feel comfortable if all four turned their eyes to me and said, you are not wise. That's probably how it can be.*
>
> (K)

Another interviewee pointed to the dynamics of the board. She de-scribed that sometimes you need to give in and that this is something to be expected if the board covers many different areas of expertise. In such a case, the social dynamics of the board will probably help to refine and articulate the intuition:

> *You have to give in, that's how it is. It is . . . it is the dynamics of . . . if a board is well composed then you get good discussions.*
>
> (B)

However, the social dynamics in the board are not always as straight-forward as in the example above. Sometimes, a board member can be hesitant to use intuition because of social dynamics that follow from a management team being successful. The quote below is a good illustration of such a situation:

> *And so I can sometimes think that—yes my gut feeling is not really like . . . oh so the management is pressing and this is a difficult question, if you have a management that normally delivers then it is much harder to say to them—no I do not think you should do it, when they really want to.*

(A)

The use of intuition could also be hindered because of the hierarchical structure of the company. One CFO described that he would always express his opinion to the CEO, well aware of the fact that the CEO made the final decision to proceed to the board. Hence, the CFO always supported the view of the CEO at the board meeting regardless of the CFO's own judgment of the financial decision to be taken:

> *I always thought that as a CFO I should always say once what I think about the thing. And if the CEO feels differently, I would continue arguing for my case. Then, finally, I would support the CEO because that's what I am there for. I can challenge things, bring my views, but at the end of the day I work for the guy, so when we go to the board, I can't have a different view anymore.*

(E)

5.6 Summary

The chapter is an account of 12 interviews with high-performing senior executives and their use of intuitive expertise in M&A financial decision-making. The interviews show that long experience, for example, being involved in many acquisitions characterizes an expert. Two areas are especially important in achieving high performance, strategic and operational expertise, and M&A expertise.

Strategic and operational expertise is related to an industry. It represents deep knowledge, gained from experience that is used when evaluating the strengths and weaknesses of a possible acquisition. M&A expertise covers the whole process, from strategic analysis to integration of the acquired company.

Almost all interviewees described that learning by "making mistakes" was crucial in their development of intuitive expertise. They also stressed that early in their careers they gained operational experience and were often challenged by a demanding task or position. In some of the cases, senior managers even let them make mistakes as a sort of learning experience. However, such an experience should always lead to an analysis of what went wrong and what was learnt.

The use of intuitive expertise to make judgments and decisions was almost always related to areas of ambiguities. Strategic investments, such as an acquisition, require a myriad of judgments that are necessary in producing the strategic and financial rationales. Usually, judgments were a result of intuitive expertise in combination with an explicit analysis. This was a typical trait of the effective use of intuitive expertise. There were also examples from the interviews of executives relying too much on the formal analysis or too much on the intuitive expertise. The worst cases, often leading to poor outcomes, seem to be when the executive uses intuition without the necessary expertise.

One reason for underreliance on intuitive expertise seems to be the presence of social dynamics. For example, at a board meeting, it can be difficult to argue from a position based on intuitive expertise, especially if all other board members have an opposing position. There were also examples of how discussions in board meetings could be hampered by the executive not being able to articulate or describe the intuition. Hence, it became "invisible" even for the expert. One way of making the intuition "visible" was to use an explicit analysis.

Notes

1 Most interviews related directly to financial decision-making in acquisitions. However, in a few interviews, other contexts were discussed, such as credit assessment and joint ventures. Arguably, these evince several similarities with financial decision-making in acquisitions.
2 The data gave us the backgrounds of the interviewees, the companies they had worked in, and the acquisitions discussed during the interviews.
3 The letter denotes the interviewee, see Appendix B. Quotes are translated from Swedish by the authors based on the transcribed interviews. In some cases, quotes are to a certain extent freely translated.
4 Discounted Cash Flow (DCF) valuation is the most widely used method for valuation of acquisition targets.

References

Dane, E., & Pratt, M.G. (2007). Exploring intuition and its role in managerial decision making. *Academy of Management Review, 32*(1), 33–54.

Ericsson, K. A., & Lehmann, A. C. (1996). Expert and exceptional performance: Evidence of maximal adaptation to task constraints. *Annual Review of Psychology, 47*(1), 273–305.

Grant, M., & Nilsson, F. (2020). The production of strategic and financial rationales in capital investments: Judgments based on intuitive expertise. *The British Accounting Review, 52*(3), 100861.

Grant, M., Nilsson, F., & Nordvall, A. C. (2020). The use of intuitive expertise in acquisition-making: An explorative study. In Sinclair, M. (Ed.). *Handbook of Intuition Research as Practice* (pp. 39–55). Cheltenham: Edward Elgar Publishing.

Kahneman, D., & Klein, G. (2009). Conditions for intuitive expertise: A failure to disagree. *American Psychologist, 64*(6), 515–526.

Polanyi, M. (2009). *The tacit dimension.* Chicago, IL: The University of Chicago Press. Originally published in 1966.

Salas, E., Rosen, M. A., & DiazGranados, D. (2010). Expertise-based intuition and decision making in organizations. *Journal of Management, 36*(4), 941–973.

Weick, K. E. (1995). *Sensemaking in organizations.* London: Sage.

6 Conclusions

In this chapter, we present a framework for intuitive expertise that summarizes our findings. Thereafter, we show how intuitive expertise applies and contributes to financial decision-making, by applying it to our empirical study and to previous field studies. Based on the contributions identified, we discuss implications for both practitioners and scholars. The book concludes with avenues for future research.

6.1 A framework for intuitive expertise

We define intuitive expertise as the capacity to intuitively "draw on our domain specific knowledge in the form of expertise accumulated in the past" (Sinclair, 2010, p. 382). This is based on a combination of intuition and expertise, as graphically illustrated in Chapter 1 (Figure 1.1).

The research by Dane and Pratt (2007, p. 40) is used to define intuition as "affectively charged judgments that arise through rapid, nonconscious, and holistic associations." Consequently, this includes intuitions with expertise as well as intuitions without expertise. Based on our review of intuition research, we describe how intuition relates to dual-process theories. In line with Hodgkinson and Sadler-Smith (2018), we argue that interactions between Type 1 intuitive processes and Type 2 reflective processes in financial decision-making are best reflected in a parallel-competitive model. The model suggests that both intuitive and analytical judgments are considered before a final judgment or decision is made. Our review of selected field studies supports this conclusion, as does our empirical study.

In defining intuition, we add to the affective component by describing the role of emotions, building on research in neuroscience (e.g., Bechara & Damasio, 2005; Bechara et al., 1997; Damasio, 1994). A conclusion from this research is that emotions are required for

DOI: 10.4324/9781003035725-6

efficient decision-making. It adds to the definition by Dane and Pratt (2007) by showing that emotions can be unconscious. Moreover, we also show that emotions can be detrimental. For example, entering a meeting in an angry state can lead to poor judgments and decisions. In contrast, positive emotional states can strengthen biases such as overconfidence (Ifcher & Zargahamee, 2014).

As described above, the definition by Dane and Pratt (2007) includes intuitions that are not based on expertise. These types of intuitions belong to the research field of heuristics and biases that examines when the use of intuitions leads to systematic errors or biases. However, in a close reading of one of the most prominent researchers in the field, Daniel Kahneman, researchers within the field seem to agree that intuitions generally are skilled and do not lead to biases (Kahneman, 2003, 2011; Tversky & Kahneman, 1974). Consequently, these findings are in line with our definition of intuitive expertise. Still, this does not preclude mistakes, for example, overconfident managers using intuition without having expertise in a domain (e.g., Kahneman, 2011; Malmendier & Tate, 2005; Roll, 1986).

We use Gobet (2016, p. 5) to define an expert as "somebody who obtains results that are vastly superior to those obtained by the majority of the population." The results (i.e., performance) should be observed over a long period of time. The definition is suitable for managerial areas, such as the domain of a university professor, a CFO, or other senior executives, in contrast to more narrow definitions used for examining expertise in laboratory experiments (e.g., Ericsson & Smith, 1991). Furthermore, we view expertise along a continuum, for example, consisting of a development along several steps from a novice to an expert (Dreyfus & Dreyfus, 1986).

We define expertise in relation to a domain and its tasks, and view a domain as typically being similar to a profession. For example, a university professor requires different knowledge and skills than that of a CFO or an auditor. Similarly, the domain of a classical piano player requires different knowledge and skills than that of a violinist. Adding to this, we describe and discuss how domains and tasks can be more or less benign for expertise (e.g., Shanteau, 1992; 2015). For example, a domain that does not lend itself to expertise is long-term political forecasts, where there are innumerable factors and events that can influence the outcome. However, domains and tasks should not be seen as static, as knowledge and tools such as IT systems and machine learning can develop domains to become more prone to expertise (Ågerfalk, 2020; Thomas & Lawrence, 2018). Furthermore, recent research argues that an individual's skilled adaption to changes is an essential part of expertise, including expertise in cases occurring with a low frequency (Ward et al., 2018).

In addition to the definition of an expert, we add knowledge about what is required to develop expertise. Genetics and environmental factors influence what one can achieve in terms of superior performance, for example, not everyone can become a Sarah Sjöström in swimming, or a Magnus Carlsen in chess. Leaving aside what we cannot influence, high-quality practice is necessary to develop expertise. Ericsson et al. (1993) use the term "deliberate practice" to describe it. According to them, activities should be adapted to the individual's existing knowledge for a long period of time, typically a decade or more. The activities should be challenging and include repetition with feedback and a gradual refinement. Thus, concentration, motivation, and persistence are required to be able to endure long periods of demanding practice. Furthermore, we show that neural and memory mechanisms can contribute to our understanding of how deliberate practice leads to the development of expertise. For example, studies in neuroscience show that practice can affect the function and structure of the brain, increasing tissue volume and connections related to the task (e.g., Maguire et al., 2000; Ullén et al., 2016). Furthermore, studies show that what we perceptually "see" and store in our memory is important for the development of expertise (e.g., De Groot 1946/1978; Chase & Simon, 1973a; Gobet, 2016). For example, experts and novices look at and remember different things: Experts see "deep structures," for example, underlying principles in physics problems, whereas novices notice "surface structures," such as visual similarities or key words (Chi et al., 1981).

After defining and consolidating the present knowledge of intuitive expertise, we examine conditions for its effectiveness. As a point of departure, we use Kahneman and Klein (2009) and how they outline two conditions for intuitive expertise, also named "skilled intuition." In describing intuitive expertise, their views on intuition and expertise are combined. They use dual-process theories and a view of skilled intuition as recognition, building on early studies of expertise in chess (Chase & Simon, 1973b; Simon, 1992). Added to this are conditions that the domain must lend itself to expertise and that people must have an opportunity to develop expertise. As Kahneman and Klein (2009, p. 520) explain: "First, the environment must provide adequately valid cues to the nature of the situation. Second, people must have an opportunity to learn the relevant cues."

To these two conditions, we add knowledge about under what circumstances, or type of tasks, the use of intuitive expertise is more effective than the use of analysis (see also Dane & Pratt, 2007). Our review suggests that for judgmental tasks the use of intuitive expertise is efficient, whereas for intellective tasks the use of analytical processes is preferred. Intellective tasks, typically, have a single answer or solution or can be broken down into subprocesses with unambiguous answers. Hence, they lend themselves to be solved analytically (Dane et al., 2012; Laughlin, 1980). Examples of these are tasks related to mathematical or engineering problems. Judgmental tasks involve judgments for which there is no single right answer or solution. These tasks have "complex underlying relationships, [with] a huge amount of data on many different variables and from many different sources, much of which covaries or is redundant" (Shapiro & Spence, 1997, p. 66). Examples of these are mergers and acquisitions and investments in R&D.

6.2 Financial decision-making and the role of intuitive expertise

In this section, we conclude what we can learn from our empirical study and the previous review of field studies about financial decision-making and the role of intuitive expertise. We do this by applying our framework of intuitive expertise.

6.2.1 Expertise

The review of field studies shows that intuitive expertise is used in financial decision-making at several levels within a company, that is, by executives and specialists. In these studies, a long period of practice in the domain (typically a decade or more) and sometimes hierarchical position were considered to be indicative of expertise. The participants in our empirical study are all senior executives, many with positions in large international companies. All of them had more than 20 years of experience, similar to the executives in the studies by Hensman and Sadler-Smith (2011) and Woiceshyn (2009). Hence, for top executives and board members, this suggests that more than two decades of experience is required to become a top performing expert. Arguably, the breadth and depth of experience and professional achievements are in these cases relevant criteria for judging the level of expertise (Hoffman, 2019). However, these characteristics should be applied with caution. As Woiceshyn (2009) shows, the "non-experts" in her study had more than two decades of experience and had reached CEO positions. Furthermore, Huang and Pearce (2015) and Huang (2018) show that for successful angel investors 10–15 years of experience seem to be sufficient.

Taken together, the empirical study and our review point in the direction that 10–20 years of experience is required to become an expert in the area of financial decision-making (e.g., Ericsson et al., 1993).

The empirical study adds to this by providing accounts of how decision-makers have developed expertise. The findings suggest that long and rich experience with exposure to challenges is important in the development of expertise. The interviews provide several examples of that, such as managing a new challenging position, or taking up a CFO position in an industry affected by radical change. Another salient finding was the importance of learning by making mistakes and having an organization that allows this. An example is how a highly successful CEO even consciously let a person make a mistake as a way to learn. In summary, these findings show that challenges and feedback were important in developing expertise (Ericsson et al., 1993).

Ericsson et al. (1993) also describe repetition as important for learning, or as Kahneman and Klein (2009, p. 520) describe it, "people must have an opportunity to learn the relevant cues." The findings from our empirical study and the field studies suggest that repetition in financial decision-making is about making judgments in changing environments. Even though there are repetitive tasks in acquisitions (Grant & Nilsson, 2020) or investments in early-stage ventures (Huang, 2018; Huang & Pearce, 2015), the environments are typically changing and different from one case to another (see Grant & Nilsson, 2020, pp. 13–14; Huang & Pearce, 2015, p. 636). Moreover, the empirical study provides several accounts of changing environments and settings for financial decision-making. This suggests, in line with recent research, that a decision-maker's skilled adaption to changes is an essential part of expertise, including expertise in cases occurring with a low frequency (Ward et al., 2018, 2020).

Finally, the empirical study provides details of two distinct areas of expertise required in financial decision-making, that is, M&A expertise and strategic and operational expertise in a specific industry. It also provides examples of failed decision-making due to lack of expertise in these areas. Furthermore, it is argued that on a board, individuals typically do not have expertise in both of these areas. Hence, it is important that board members together cover expertise in the areas required.

6.2.2 Use of intuition and analysis

The review of field studies shows that financial decision-making is about the use of both intuitive expertise and analysis. The empirical study adds to this finding by providing detailed accounts of how experts use intuitive and analytical judgments. Strategic reasons, largely based on analysis, were typically an important starting point for a financial decision. Subsequently, intuitive expertise was used in judgmental tasks such as assessing synergies, financial forecasts, and valuation. This is similar to what Huang (2018) calls the "control-focused" stance, where decision-making starts with analysis followed by an intuitively led process. However, the so-called "choice-based" stance starting in an intuitive process followed by analysis could also be discerned for some interviewees. Suggestively, the stance that the expert chooses depends to a certain degree on individual characteristics. However, in line with our review, findings suggest that before a final judgment or decision is made, both intuitive and analytical judgments are considered.

The use of intuitive expertise for the judgment of people was a salient finding in both the review and the empirical study. Several of the studies also suggest that it is critical for the outcome of decision-making. For example, Lipshitz and Shulimovitz (2007) show how the use of intuitive expertise in judging loan applicants efficiently identifies problematic credit status. Another example is Huang and Pearce (2015), who demonstrate how intuitive judgments about the entrepreneur's ability more accurately predict the outcome of investments in early ventures than analytical judgments. The empirical study supports this and provides further examples. It shows that all interviewees described the intuitive judgments of people as critical in financial decision-making. This finding relates to the assessment of the management and key personnel set to manage the acquisition and its integration, including having managers present the strategic decision to the board.

Financial decision-making is, to a large extent, focused on the future development of the investment and its environment. These examples concern the assessment of people managing the business in the future, for example, an entrepreneur or a manager integrating an acquisition. How the future will take shape, for example as described in financial forecasts and underlying assumptions about the environment, is highly uncertain, and a myriad of unanticipated changes will likely occur after an investment has been made. Consequently, intuitive judgments assess peoples' abilities to manage unanticipated changes in the future. As Huang and Pearce (2015) demonstrate, even in decision-making under extreme risk intuitive judgments provide efficient guidance to make this assessment, and they arguably manage risk.

Further, the empirical study contributes to a more complete picture of how intuitive expertise is used by specialists and decision-makers.

In an earlier study by us, we describe how specialists assigned to make acquisitions use intuitive expertise in the production of strategic and financial rationales; however, for producing decision documents, analytical reasoning dominates (Grant & Nilsson, 2020). Similarly, we show how specialists use intuitive judgments in negotiations and due diligence (Grant et al., 2020). The present empirical study shows that at the board level decision-makers use intuitive judgments not only to assess the decision documents, but also to judge the specialists presenting them. Hence, the empirical study adds to our earlier studies (Grant & Nilsson, 2020; Grant et al., 2020) by showing that decision-makers intuitively assess specialists and the specialists' intuitive judgment.

6.2.3 Effectiveness of the use of intuitive expertise in financial decision-making

The reviewed field studies and the empirical study provide strong support for financial decision-making as a domain benign for expertise. They even include professional "angel investors" who invest in start-ups with extreme risks. As described in the previous sections, an important part of this expertise seems to be the ability to assess the individuals being a part of realizing the investment and their abilities to manage the future, for example, unexpected changes.

Angel investors expect that most of their investments will not be profitable, whereas a few will be very profitable. However, taken together, their portfolio of investments is expected to be profitable (Huang, 2018; Huang & Pearce, 2015). The empirical study provides examples of a parallel to this reasoning. Interviewees described investments in new technology companies as highly uncertain. A way to manage such a situation was to make smaller investments in several companies and treat them as an R&D portfolio, expecting only some of them to succeed.

The review and the empirical study strongly support that intuitive expertise is used for judgmental tasks. The studies provide a rich account of the use of intuitive expertise on tasks that lack unambiguous answers or solutions. To a large extent, these tasks are related to the future. For example: Will this company be able to repay its loans? Will this entrepreneur be able to build a successful business? Another example is from the empirical study, showing how board members use intuitive expertise to judge board documents with financial forecasts, the valuation and synergy plans, and the managers responsible for managing the acquisition and its integration.

In summary, the review and empirical study shows that intuitive expertise plays a critical role in financial decision-making. This conclusion is supported by studies directly following up the outcome of the use of intuitive expertise (Grant & Nilsson, 2020; Huang & Pearce, 2015; Lipshitz & Schulimovitz, 2007). Furthermore, in all studies, the findings meet the conditions for effective use outlined in our framework, that is, the domain lends itself to expertise, expertise is present, and the character of the task is judgmental and thus more efficiently solved with the use of intuitive expertise than with analysis.

However, even if the studies show the effective use of intuitive expertise, the empirical study also provides some examples of poor investments caused by over- and underreliance on intuitive expertise, as well as the lack of expertise. For example, one of the interviewees described that he sometimes had directly relied on the intuitive judgment without checking the facts. This example is in line with the view of people being cognitive misers and relying on the first intuitive answer without checking it analytically (Kahneman, 2011), perhaps caused by overconfidence (Kahneman, 2011; Malmendier & Tate, 2005). There were also examples of poor outcomes caused by people not relying enough on intuitive expertise. One interviewee described that his intuition had said no, but he was not able to articulate this in analytical terms. The acquisition was approved but later turned out to be a failure. Interviewees also provided several examples of poor acquisitions caused by lack of expertise. For example, one interviewee described an acquisition in an industry where he and the other senior executives had knowledge about the industry and the products. However, what became clear after the acquisition was that they lacked deep strategic and operational knowledge about the industry and products, and the acquisition proved to be a failure. Overconfidence is perhaps one explanation for this example and other accounts of poor investments in the empirical study (Kahneman, 2011; Malmendier & Tate, 2005).

6.3 Implications and future research

The role of intuitive expertise in financial decision-making has so far attracted rather limited interest among both scholars and practitioners in the fields of accounting and finance. This is surprising, and it is difficult to explain the reason for it. How judgments and decisions are made is of fundamental importance to our understanding of human behavior and is an important research field not only in psychology but also in management. In accounting and finance, the interest seems to be directed more toward how rational decision-making can be supported by using formal models and tools. Less interest is directed toward judgments and decisions that are difficult to discern. They almost become invisible and are, therefore, hard to study with traditional methods. Intuition, even when combined with expertise, is also a human trait that is looked upon with suspicion by some scholars and practitioners. They seem to connect intuition with guessing, sloppiness, and other traits that are not considered relevant to decision-making by high-performing senior executives. Our book shows that such an attitude risks missing out the finer details of how financial decision-making is actually done in practice and that intuitive expertise does not undermine rational decision-making. Instead, we claim that it is an important characteristic that high-performing senior executives possess. From that position, several implications can be identified.

Starting with implications for practitioners, one take-away is that the importance of talent to become an expert is often exaggerated. Of course, there can be an upper limit to what one can achieve, but deliberate practice, in combination with motivation and endurance, is much more important. Therefore, the development from being a novice to becoming an expert is dependent on your focus on building deep knowledge in a specific domain. That process of learning is dependent on context, or, in other words, the extent to which you are constantly pushed to test the limits of your knowledge. There is also a need to have a solid understanding of the models and tools that support financial decision-making. It seems like the expert has acquired such a deep understanding that the models and tools are used primarily to explain to others how judgments and decisions have been made. For scholars, these insights have implications for both research and education. Perhaps most important is the need to identify what type of knowledge is necessary to prepare students for the journey from being a novice to becoming an expert. Solid knowledge of accounting is necessary, but this knowledge must also be applied in realistic real-world situations. Therefore, we believe that much more research should be directed toward understanding what expertise in accounting consists of, how it is developed, and the role of universities in that process.

Even though we are convinced of the importance of intuitive expertise in financial decision-making, this book is the result of an ongoing research endeavor. The findings are explorative and, hence, preliminary. We will continue to do research in the area for a long time, and we see many promising avenues for future research. One such area is how auditors develop and use intuitive expertise. This is a fascinating domain to study, since the development from an audit associate to a senior partner is very much related to the expertise acquired by deliberate practice. Another promising area is how fund managers use intuitive expertise when deciding what investments to pursue. We find this domain interesting, because the literature in the field has a very strong focus on the design and the use of formal models and less on the experts making the decisions. These are only two examples based on our current research interests, and there are of course many more areas that we need to study. We hope this book can serve as an inspiration to scholars and practitioners who want to contribute to enhancing our knowledge of the role of intuitive expertise in financial decision-making.

References

Ågerfalk, P. J. (2020). Artificial intelligence as digital agency. *European Journal of Information Systems, 29*(1), 1–8.

Bechara, A., & Damasio, A. R. (2005). The somatic marker hypothesis: A neural theory of economic decision. *Games and Economic Behavior, 52*(2), 336–372.

Bechara, A., Damasio, H., Tranel, D., & Damasio, A. R. (1997). Deciding advantageously before knowing the advantageous strategy. *Science, 275*(5304), 1293–1295.

Chase, W. G., & Simon, H. A. (1973a). Perception in chess. *Cognitive Psychology, 4*(1), 55–81.

Chase, W. G., & Simon, H. A. (1973b). The mind's eye in chess. In Chase W. G. (Ed.), *Visual Information Processing* (pp. 215–281). New York, NY: Academic Press.

Chi, M. T., Feltovich, P. J., & Glaser, R. (1981). Categorization and representation of physics problems by experts and novices. *Cognitive Science, 5*(2), 121–152.

Damasio, A. R. (1994). *Descartes' error: Emotion, reason, and the human brain.* New York, NY: Grosset/Putnam.

Dane, E., & Pratt, M. G. (2007). Exploring intuition and its role in managerial decision making. *Academy of Management Review, 32*(1), 33–54.

Dane, E., Rockmann, K. W., & Pratt, M. G. (2012). When should I trust my gut? Linking domain expertise to intuitive decision-making effectiveness. *Organizational Behavior and Human Decision Processes, 119*(2), 187–194.

De Groot, A. D. (1978). *Thought and choice in chess* (2nd ed.) (first Dutch edition in 1946). The Hague: Mouton Publishers.

Dreyfus, H. L., & Dreyfus, S. E. (1986). *Mind over machine – The Power of human intuition and expertise in the era of the computer.* New York, NY: The Free Press.

Ericsson, K. A., Krampe, R. T., & Tesch-Römer, C. (1993). The role of deliberate practice in the acquisition of expert performance. *Psychological Review, 100*(3), 363–406.

Ericsson, K. A., & Smith, J. (1991). *Toward a general theory of expertise: Prospects and limits.* Cambridge: Cambridge University Press.

Gobet, F. (2016). *Understanding expertise: A multi-disciplinary approach.* London: Red Globe Press.

Grant, M., & Nilsson, F. (2020). The production of strategic and financial rationales in capital investments: Judgments based on intuitive expertise. *The British Accounting Review, 52*(3), 100861.

Grant, M., Nilsson, F., & Nordvall, A. C. (2020). The use of intuitive expertise in acquisition-making: An explorative study. In Sinclair, M. (Ed.), *Handbook of Intuition Research as Practice* (pp. 39–55). Cheltenham: Edward Elgar Publishing.

Hensman, A., & Sadler-Smith, E. (2011). Intuitive decision making in banking and finance. *European Management Journal, 29*(1), 51–66.

Hodgkinson, G. P., & Sadler-Smith, E. (2018). The dynamics of intuition and analysis in managerial and organizational decision making. *Academy of Management Perspectives, 32*(4), 473–492.

Hoffman, R. R. (2019). Identifying experts for the design of human-centered systems, downloaded October 10, 2021, from https://www.ihmc.us/hoffmans-concept-blog/.

Huang, L. (2018). The role of investor gut feel in managing complexity and extreme risk. *Academy of Management Journal, 61*(5), 1821–1847.

Huang, L., & Pearce, J. L. (2015). Managing the unknowable: The effectiveness of early-stage investor gut feel in entrepreneurial investment decisions. *Administrative Science Quarterly, 60*(4), 634–670.

Ifcher, J., & Zarghamee, H. (2014). Affect and overconfidence: A laboratory investigation. *Journal of Neuroscience, Psychology, and Economics, 7*(3), 125–150.

Kahneman, D. (2003). A perspective on judgment and choice: Mapping bounded rationality. *American Psychologist, 58*(9), 697–720.

Kahneman, D. (2011). *Thinking, fast and slow.* New York, NY: Farrar, Straus and Giroux.

Kahneman, D., & Klein, G. (2009). Conditions for intuitive expertise: A failure to disagree. *American Psychologist, 64*(6), 515–526.

Laughlin, P. R. (1980). Social combination processes of cooperative problem-solving groups on verbal intellective tasks. In Fishbein, M. (Ed.). *Progress in Social Psychology* (vol. 1, pp. 127–155). Hillsdale, NJ: Lawrence Erlbaum Associates.

Lipshitz, R., & Shulimovitz, N. (2007). Intuition and emotion in bank loan officers' credit decisions. *Journal of Cognitive Engineering and Decision Making, 1*(2), 212–233.

Maguire, E. A., Gadian, D. G., Johnsrude, I. S., Good, C. D., Ashburner, J., Frackowiak, R. S., & Frith, C. D. (2000). Navigation-related structural change in the hippocampi of taxi drivers. *Proceedings of the National Academy of Sciences, 97*(8), 4398–4403.

Malmendier, U., & Tate, G. (2005). CEO overconfidence and corporate investment. *The Journal of Finance, 60*(6), 2661–2700.

Roll, R. (1986). The hubris hypothesis of corporate takeovers. *Journal of Business*, *59*(2), 197–216.

Shanteau, J. (1992). Competence in experts: The role of task characteristics. *Organizational Behavior and Human Decision Processes*, *53*(2), 252–266.

Shanteau, J. (2015). Why task domains (still) matter for understanding expertise. *Journal of Applied Research in Memory and Cognition*, *4*(3), 169–175.

Shapiro, S., & Spence, M. T. (1997). Managerial intuition: A conceptual and operational framework. *Business Horizons*, *40*(1), 63–69.

Simon, H. A. (1992). What is an "explanation" of behavior? *Psychological Science*, *3*(3), 150–161.

Sinclair, M. (2010). Misconceptions about intuition. *Psychological Inquiry*, *21*(4), 378–386.

Thomas, R. P., & Lawrence, A. (2018). Assessment of expert performance compared across professional domains. *Journal of Applied Research in Memory and Cognition*, *7*(2), 167–176.

Tversky, A., & Kahneman, D. (1974). Judgment under uncertainty: Heuristics and biases. *Science*, *185*(4157), 1124–1131.

Ullén, F., Hambrick, D. Z., & Mosing, M. A. (2016). Rethinking expertise: A multifactorial gene–environment interaction model of expert performance. *Psychological Bulletin*, *142*(4), 427–446.

Ward, P., Gore, J., Hutton, R., Conway, G. E., & Hoffman, R. R. (2018). Adaptive skill as the conditio sine qua non of expertise. *Journal of Applied Research in Memory and Cognition*, *7*(1), 35–50.

Ward, P., Schraagen, J. M., Gore, J., & Roth, E. M. (Eds.). (2020). *The Oxford handbook of expertise*. Oxford: Oxford University Press.

Woiceshyn, J. (2009). Lessons from "good minds": How CEOs use intuition, analysis and guiding principles to make strategic decisions. *Long Range Planning*, *42*(3), 298–319.

Appendix A
Methods

The empirical study is based on interviews with 12 high-performing senior executives. All of them have more than 20 years of experience in senior positions (their background and other relevant data are presented in Appendix B). They all have backgrounds, experience, and track records that make them well qualified as experts in M&A financial decision-making. The interviewees were identified from our deep knowledge of Swedish industry in general and the M&A community in particular. The interviews were complemented with additional data, for example, annual reports, company websites, and articles in the business press.

The interviews were semi-structured and recorded. In most cases, they were held via Zoom but in one case a mobile phone was used. The interviews were held in Swedish, except one, which was held in English. Below are examples of the areas covered in the interviews:

- The use of intuitive expertise when judging a potential acquisition target (e.g., in which situations was intuitive expertise vs. more of structured and explicit analysis used?).
- Examples of M&A or other investment projects, in which intuitive expertise was especially important and why (e.g., intuitive expertise vs. structured and explicit analysis).
- Examples of M&A or other investment projects in which:
  - intuitive expertise was in conflict with a structured and explicit analysis;
  - one should have relied more on intuitive expertise; and
  - intuitive expertise led to a bad decision.
- Openness in using intuitive expertise.
- The characteristics of an expert in financial decision-making.
- The development of expertise.

The interviews were transcribed by a third party. The transcribed interviews were analyzed by going back and forth between the literature, themes, ideas, and data. In the first stage of the analysis, one of the authors read each interview, listened to tapes, and searched for archival data related to each interviewee. Based on this analysis, broad themes were identified together with relevant quotes and archival data. The tangible result was a document consisting of more than 100 pages.

In the second stage of the analysis, the document was read and analyzed again. New quotes and insights were added. Moreover, the archival data were further analyzed. The result of this was refined themes and the addition of new themes.

In the third stage, the results were further refined. This was an iterative process moving back and forth between the themes identified, the interviews, and archival data. This resulted in final themes that were further divided into subthemes.

The final result of stages 1–3 can be found in Chapter 5, that is, a detailed account of the findings from the empirical study. There is also a separate document of 45 pages consisting of supporting data for each theme and subtheme.

Although the study contributes to the understanding of the use of intuitive expertise in financial decision-making, the study has several limitations. First, it is based on a limited number of interviews, using retrospective accounts. Hence, future studies could use larger samples and other methods such as think-aloud protocols to improve the validity of the findings. Second, the interviewees were selected based on the criteria of having long experience and holding senior positions. Furthermore, all the interviewees seemed to fulfill the criteria of deliberate learning. Additional studies could refine and add criteria to strengthen the selection of experts. Third, performance of the use of intuitive expertise was based on the interviewees' own statements. The secondary data could confirm some of the examples described as having poor outcomes. However, successful use of intuitive expertise was inferred by the position and reputation of the interviewee and the companies that the interviewee worked in. Thus, future studies could use other methods to follow up the performance of the use of intuitive expertise in greater detail.

Appendix B
Description of interviewees

A	Industry expertise: > 20 years in the telecom industries. M&A expertise: Worked closely with acquisitions, and long-time board member in a highly acquisitive and successful company. Expertise in assessing M&A capabilities, including integration capabilities. Board experience: Experience from 28 boards. Is currently active on 14 boards.
B	Industry expertise: > 20 years in advisory roles (e.g., audit and accounting) M&A expertise: Worked as an M&A adviser. Audit and accounting expertise. Expertise in assessing M&A capabilities, including integration capabilities. Board experience: Is currently active on eight boards.
C	Industry expertise: > 20 years in the telecom and IT industries. M&A expertise: Investment expertise. Previous CEO, board member, and industrial adviser to private equity. Board experience: Experience from six boards. Is currently active on five boards.
D	Industry expertise: > 20 years as a financial adviser. M&A expertise: Investment banker, financial adviser (own company), and board member. Board experience: Experience from nine boards. Is currently active on five boards.
E	Industry expertise: > 20 years in telecom and media industries. M&A expertise: Plentiful, especially in telecom. Board experience: Experience from seven boards. Is currently active on four boards.
F	Industry expertise: > 20 years in very large manufacturing industries. M&A expertise: Being a CFO in several serial acquirers. Board experience: Experience from one board.

G	Industry expertise: > 20 years mainly in the vehicle-manufacturing industry. M&A expertise: Being a CFO in very large companies. Board experience: Experience from one board.
H	Industry expertise: > 20 years in the banking industry. M&A expertise: Participated in two large acquisitions. Board experience: Experience from one board.
I	Industry experience: > 20 years from the banking industry and several other industries. M&A expertise: CEO, CFO, president, and board member in very large companies. Board experience: Experience from many boards.
J	Industry expertise: > 20 years from telecom and other industries. M&A expertise: As CEO and CFO in very large companies. Board experience: Experience from six boards. Is currently active on six boards.
K	Industry expertise: > 20 years in the banking industry. M&A expertise: As CFO. Expert in credit assessment. Board experience: Experience from eight boards. Is currently active on six boards.
L	Industry expertise: > 20 years in manufacturing industry. M&A expertise: As CFO in a very large acquisitive company. Board experience: Currently active on three boards.

Index

Printed in the United States
by Baker & Taylor Publisher Services